Whooping Cough

Titles in the Diseases & Disorders series include:

DISEASES & DISORDERS

Whooping Cough

Toney Allman

LUCENT BOOKS
A part of Gale, Cengage Learning

GALE
CENGAGE Learning

Detroit • New York • San Francisco • New Haven, Conn • Waterville, Maine • London

© 2012 Gale, Cengage Learning

LIBRARY OF CONGRESS CATALOGING-IN-PUBLICATION DATA

Allman, Toney.
  Whooping cough / by Toney Allman.
    p. cm. -- (Diseases and disorders)
  Summary: "This series objectively and thoughtfully explores topics of medical importance. Books include sections on a description of the disease or disorder and how it affects the body, as well as diagnosis and treatment of the condition"-- Provided by publisher.
  Includes bibliographical references and index.
  ISBN 978-1-4205-0736-2 (hardback)
  1. Whooping cough--Juvenile literature. I. Title.
  RC204.A45 2012
    616.2'04--dc23
                                                    2011046860

Lucent Books
27500 Drake Rd.
Farmington Hills, MI 48331

ISBN-13: 978-1-4205-0736-2
ISBN-10: 1-4205-0736-2

Printed in the United States of America
2 3 4 5 6 7 16 15 14 13 12

Table of Contents

"The Most Difficult Puzzles Ever Devised"

Charles Best, one of the pioneers in the search for a cure for diabetes, once explained what it is about medical research that intrigued him so. "It's not just the gratification of knowing one is helping people," he confided, "although that probably is a more heroic and selfless motivation. Those feelings may enter in, but truly, what I find best is the feeling of going toe to toe with nature, of trying to solve the most difficult puzzles ever devised. The answers are there somewhere, those keys that will solve the puzzle and make the patient well. But how will those keys be found?"

Since the dawn of civilization, nothing has so puzzled people—and often frightened them, as well—as the onset of illness in a body or mind that had seemed healthy before. A seizure, the inability of a heart to pump, the sudden deterioration of muscle tone in a small child—being unable to reverse such conditions or even to understand why they occur was unspeakably frustrating to healers. Even before there were names for such conditions, even before they were understood at all, each was a reminder of how complex the human body was, and how vulnerable.

While our grappling with understanding diseases has been frustrating at times, it has also provided some of humankind's most heroic accomplishments. Alexander Fleming's accidental discovery in 1928 of a mold that could be turned into penicillin has resulted in the saving of untold millions of lives. The isolation of the enzyme insulin has reversed what was once a death sentence for anyone with diabetes. There have been great strides in combating conditions for which there is not yet a cure, too. Medicines can help AIDS patients live longer, diagnostic tools such as mammography and ultrasounds can help doctors find tumors while they are treatable, and laser surgery techniques have made the most intricate, minute operations routine.

This "toe-to-toe" competition with diseases and disorders is even more remarkable when seen in a historical continuum. An astonishing amount of progress has been made in a very short time. Just two hundred years ago, the existence of germs as a cause of some diseases was unknown. In fact, it was less than 150 years ago that a British surgeon named Joseph Lister had difficulty persuading his fellow doctors that washing their hands before delivering a baby might increase the chances of a healthy delivery (especially if they had just attended to a diseased patient)!

Each book in Lucent's Diseases and Disorders series explores a disease or disorder and the knowledge that has been accumulated (or discarded) by doctors through the years. Each book also examines the tools used for pinpointing a diagnosis, as well as the various means that are used to treat or cure a disease. Finally, new ideas are presented—techniques or medicines that may be on the horizon.

Frustration and disappointment are still part of medicine, for not every disease or condition can be cured or prevented. But the limitations of knowledge are being pushed outward constantly; the "most difficult puzzles ever devised" are finding challengers every day.

The Hundred-Day Cough

Whooping cough was once a common and greatly feared childhood disease. With no way to prevent or treat it, parents and doctors could do little more than hope that an infected baby would not die. Throughout the first half of the twentieth century, thousands of young children died each year, while infected older children, teens, and adults suffered through months of illness. Then, medical researchers learned how to prevent whooping cough with a vaccine. Doctors offered parents the vaccine to protect their children, and parents gratefully accepted. By the 1970s, whooping cough seemed to be a disease of the past. No one feared getting whooping cough anymore. Today, however, whooping cough has returned. Around the world in communities and populations that had almost forgotten about it, people are again learning about this rather old-fashioned yet dangerous illness that the Chinese once aptly named the "hundred-day cough."

The Return of Whooping Cough

Pediatrician Margaret Morris of North Carolina's Chapel Hill Children's Clinic explains what makes whooping cough such an ordeal:

> There are coughs and there are coughs. Some are annoyances, some signify important health problems, some interfere with sleep. But few coughing illnesses can compare

with whooping cough, a disease that had become uncommon but that is now making a comeback. It is exhausting to have a cough for a few days. But whooping cough has been called the 100 day cough. Can you handle one that lasts for months, or watch your child in an awesome display of desperation and air hunger as he tries to fit a breath of air into the paroxysm [fit] of coughing? Over and over, day after day, the whoop, the exhaustion. It's a scary disease and can be a deadly disease, especially for the very young. Whooping cough is back.[1]

No one has to tell Samantha, an Iowa teen, that whooping cough is back. When she was fifteen years old, Samantha got whooping cough and suffered prolonged bouts of coughing—day after day—for weeks. She could not sleep at night. Her chest hurt. She felt as if she could not breathe, and she often vomited at the end of a coughing spell. Eating seemed to make her cough, so she ate very little. At first, her doctor placed Samantha under quarantine—he told her not to leave the

A Victorian-era medical trade card touts supposed cures for colds, coughs, asthma, and whooping cough. Whooping cough killed thousands of children in the nineteenth and early twentieth centuries.

house for five days so that she would not give the disease to anyone else. Once the quarantine was over, Samantha returned to school, but she was still far from well. Her mother recalls, "After her quarantine, Samantha went back to school, despite the difficulties her condition created. Simple things that she took for granted, like going up and down the stairs, became a real chore. Activities that used to be fun, like gym class, became a struggle to breathe."[2]

Danger Ahead

Samantha eventually recovered from her bout with whooping cough, but stories such as hers are becoming increasingly common in the United States and other countries throughout the world. Many doctors and medical researchers worry that whooping cough's return could mean serious trouble if the rising rates of infection cannot be stemmed. Whether the disease will become a problem again or new discoveries will again reduce it to a nonissue remains to be seen.

CHAPTER ONE

What Is Whooping Cough?

In February 2009 Jude (her real name has been withheld to protect her privacy), a thirty-four-year-old woman from Brisbane, Australia, learned what whooping cough is. Jude was preparing for her honeymoon when the symptoms of sickness began. At first, she was not very ill. She was just tired and had no energy. She had a fever and a dry cough. When she visited her doctor, he thought she had the flu or bronchitis and prescribed antibiotics. The medicine did no good, and while on her honeymoon, Jude got sicker. Her dry cough became long coughing spells that made her feel as if she could not catch her breath. One night she woke up coughing so badly that she thought she was dying. When the long series of coughs stopped and she tried to take a breath, she heard a whooping noise. She remembers, "I could barely, barely suck air into a small pinprick sized gap in my throat." She and her husband did not know what to do. They were in a strange city in the middle of the night, so when the coughing spell eased, they went back to sleep. Then, Jude recalls, "a few hours later, while browsing a local arts and crafts market I had another cough with the strange throat swelling feeling and I gasped for as much air as I could get into that pinprick sized breathing space in my throat."[3] That was when Jude went to the hospital emergency room. She was given medicine to reduce the inflammation in her throat, but she still did not find out what was wrong with her.

The Long Ordeal

By the time the couple returned home from their honeymoon, Jude was scared and exhausted from her repeated coughing spells. She was bringing up lots of clear, thick mucus, or phlegm, when she coughed, and sometimes the coughing led to vomiting. Her doctor finally ran a blood test for whooping cough, and the test came back positive. There was little he could do for her because there is no treatment that can cure whooping cough. He did give her a different antibiotic to take so she would not infect other people, but it could not change the course of her whooping cough. The doctor told Jude that she would recover but that she might be sick for as long as three months. So Jude learned to cope with her illness. For the first month of her sickness, Jude's doctor ordered her to stay home from work. He explained that the germs, or bacteria, that cause whooping cough are catching, and she had to stay away from other people until her course of antibiotics was finished so as not to give others the disease. Jude stayed home and suffered spasms of coughing four or five times a day. They often left her so exhausted that all she could do was lie on the couch all day trying to recover from the spells. She learned to sleep upright in a chair, to breathe steam through a vaporizer, to take lots of hot showers, and to avoid eating or drinking anything cold. All of these things helped to reduce the thick mucus that choked her and made breathing so difficult.

By the second month, because of the antibiotic she was taking, Jude was no longer likely to give her whooping cough to others, so the doctor allowed her to return to work part-time. Jude's coughing spells had changed, too. They were deep and loud, and she was bringing up thick, green phlegm when she coughed. She still gasped in panic during the coughing spasms and had to remind herself to relax as she struggled to breathe. She had little energy. She worked about four hours a day and

Whooping cough symptoms include repeated, prolonged coughing spells that produce heavy mucus, or phlegm, and that may lead to chronic vomiting.

then went home and slept the rest of the day. On some days, she did not go to work at all but slept the entire day. By the end of this period, however, the coughing spasms began to ease and become less severe. Jude remembers that by mid-April, the third month of her illness, she began to see that the end of the ordeal was in sight. She was still coughing but not in long spasms. She was able to go back to sleeping in her bed. She could work six hours a day without exhaustion, and she began walking for exercise. On some days, she still felt miserable and exhausted, but the illness had finally run its course. By the end of April, Jude coughed only occasionally. She was able to ride her bicycle again, had the energy to work full-time, and was feeling normal. She wrote in her journal, "Feeling soooo much better. Promise never to take health for granted again!"[4] Her body did remain weak for a few more months, and she easily caught colds and minor illnesses until she grew stronger, but she eventually recovered completely from her long ordeal.

Whooping Cough Around the World

Jude had never known anyone who had whooping cough, but she is far from alone in her difficult experience. Around the world, according to the Centers for Disease Control and Prevention (CDC), a U.S. public health agency, as many as 50 million people suffer with the disease each year, mostly in poorer, developing countries. People in developed countries, however, are at risk for the disease, too. The CDC reports that seventeen thousand people in the United States and twice that many in Australia came down with whooping cough in 2009. More than twenty-thousand cases were reported in Europe in 2008, and about twenty-five hundred cases occur each year in Canada. Most adults and young people over the age of about ten recover from whooping cough, but for infants and young children the disease is particularly dangerous. The CDC says that about three hundred thousand people around the world die of whooping cough every year, most of them young children.

Approximately 92 percent of whooping cough deaths are in infants less than four months old. Natalie Norton, for example, a resident of Hawaii, lost her infant son Gavin to whooping

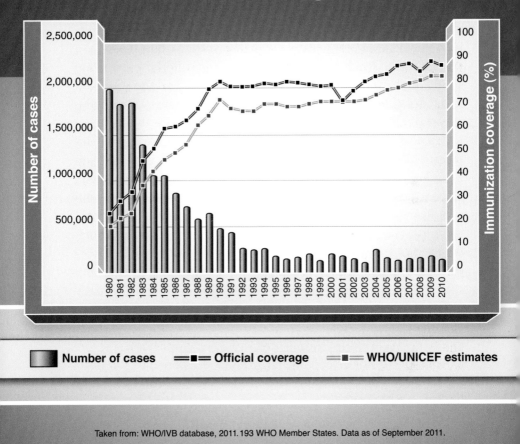

Pertussis Global Annual Reported Cases and DTP3 Coverage, 1980–2010

Number of cases   ■ **Official coverage**   ■ **WHO/UNICEF estimates**

Taken from: WHO/IVB database, 2011. 193 WHO Member States. Data as of September 2011.

cough. Although Gavin was hospitalized and received good medical care, he could not fight off the disease. His mother recalls, "It was a very quick decline. He was very ill and it was fast and it was terrible. We watched him die from pertussis."[5]

The Stages of Whooping Cough

Whooping cough's medical name is pertussis. It is an infectious disease that is caught from other people, just as people catch colds from one another. It is caused by a bacterium that invades the body and attacks the airways and lungs. It is commonly called whooping cough because of the whooping sound

that victims make when they gasp for air at the end of a prolonged spasm of coughing. Although not everyone has exactly
the same symptoms, the course of the illness is usually quite
similar to what Jude described in her journal.

Medical experts generally divide the course of pertussis into
three stages. The first stage of pertussis is called the catarrhal
stage. *Catarrhal* means "containing mucus," and the word *ca-*
tarrh describes an inflammation of mucous membranes in the
upper respiratory tract or air passages, including the nose, si-
nuses, and throat. Catarrhal symptoms are typical of the common cold. They include a runny nose, sneezing, mild fever, and
a mild cough. The catarrhal stage of pertussis lasts about seven
to ten days, and during this period, explains the CDC, the
symptoms are "indistinguishable from those of minor respiratory infections." The CDC refers to this stage as an "insidious
onset"[6] because neither the infected person nor his or her doctor recognizes that a serious illness is beginning or that any
special treatment is necessary. The disease develops gradually
and looks like a minor infection such as a cold.

The first stage of pertussis is called the catarrhal stage. This is an
inflammation of the mucous membranes in the upper respiratory
tract, or air passages, that creates mucus, or sputum.

Unlike minor illnesses, however, pertussis moves into the second stage within one to two weeks, as the symptom of coughing gradually gets worse. The second stage is named the paroxysmal stage. Paroxysms are fits of prolonged coughing. This stage can last anywhere from a week to ten weeks. It is characterized by paroxysmal attacks that occur, on average, about fifteen times a day, usually in the evening or at night. Doctors and researchers believe that the paroxysms are due to the difficulty of bringing up and expelling the thick mucus that has developed in the lungs, trachea (windpipe), and bronchi (tubes that branch off into the lungs) of the respiratory tract. At the end of a paroxysm, the characteristic, high-pitched whoop of pertussis occurs in about 50 percent of victims. Infants less than about six months of age often do not have the strength to whoop, but they do have the prolonged coughing spasms. Instead of the whoop, they may choke and experience apnea—that is, they stop breathing for at least twenty seconds. During the paroxysmal attack, adults as well as infants and young children may appear cyanotic—that is, they turn blue from lack of oxygen. Adults and older children usually gasp soon enough that they do not have apnea and so may not develop cyanosis. Instead, their faces may turn red with exertion, their eyes may bulge, and their tongues may protrude. Most people report feeling that they cannot breathe, and because of this they become anxious and frightened. Victims of all ages commonly vomit after an attack because of gagging on the heavy amount of fluid and mucus that is produced. Almost all victims are exhausted after the attack, and according to experts, infants appear particularly distressed.

Generally, the coughing attacks of the paroxysmal stage worsen during the first couple of weeks, then stay the same for about 3 weeks, and finally begin to decrease gradually during the last 1 to 2 weeks. Then the patient enters the last stage of whooping cough—the convalescent stage. This stage usually lasts about 2 to 4 weeks, but in some cases, it may go on for months. During the convalescent stage, the person gradually experiences fewer and fewer paroxysms of coughing and has less and less thick mucus in the airway. Like Jude, people in the

Before Symptoms Appear

The time between catching an infectious disease and the appearance of its first symptoms is called the incubation period. In whooping cough, this period is usually between 7 and 10 days, but it can be as short as 4 days or, rarely, as long as 42 days. During the incubation period, the disease-causing bacteria are penetrating the tissues in the respiratory tract but are not yet causing any symptoms. This means that the person has whooping cough but does not yet know it. It also means that by the time symptoms appear, an individual may not remember having been exposed to someone's coughing days or weeks before, so people with whooping cough often do not know how they caught the disease. With some diseases, people can spread the germs to others during the incubation period, but whooping cough is usually spread during the catarrhal and paroxysmal stages of the disease.

Shown here is a light micrograph image of the bacterium *Bordetella pertussis* (*B. pertussis*), which causes whooping cough.

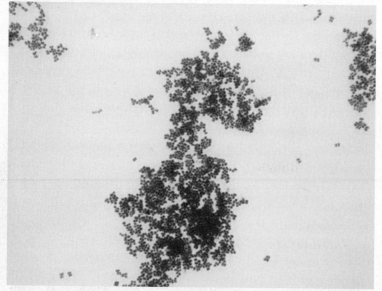

convalescent stage begin to feel better and to have more energy. Eventually the paroxysms and mucus disappear, although bouts of nonparoxysmal coughing may continue for several more weeks after that. Even when the last stage of the disease is over, however, the CDC says that the paroxysms may return at any time over many subsequent months should the victim catch a respiratory infection, such as a cold.

Mild Whooping Cough

The severity and duration of the three stages of whooping cough can vary, depending on individual circumstances. Most adults, for instance, were vaccinated as infants or children to protect them from coming down with whooping cough. The protection diminishes over time, but even some residual or leftover protection can mean a mild case of pertussis for many adults and teens who are infected. The staff of the Mayo Clinic notes, "Sometimes, a persistent hacking cough is the only sign that an adolescent or adult has whooping cough."[7] These patients may not develop the whoop or the vomiting that is characteristic of a more serious case of pertussis. They may not experience the thick phlegm that fills the windpipe and makes breathing so difficult. Nevertheless, even mild cases of whooping cough can be difficult and uncomfortable.

Jane Walden, a florist and mother of two in Nottingham, England, got whooping cough in 2002. She thought she just had a particularly severe cold, but after about ten days of feeling ill, her coughs became long fits of coughing that lasted several minutes at a time, especially at night. She says it felt as if something was stuck down in her chest. She remembers it "being worse at night; the coughing really started to disrupt my sleep. I'd prop myself up in bed in an attempt to stop the fits, but it made no difference. Even the bottles of cough medicine I went through did nothing but [waste my money]. The cough dragged on for nearly eight weeks before I started to feel a bit better."[8] Walden did not see a doctor and did not know she had had whooping cough until her seven-year-old daughter, Emily, began to experience the same symptoms. Emily coughed so hard that she turned red in the face and gasped for breath. When

Walden took Emily to the doctor, he explained that both mother and daughter had what he called mild whooping cough.

Not everyone who gets pertussis is as fortunate as the Waldens. Terrell, for example, is a middle-aged man who was vaccinated as a child but later caught whooping cough from his wife. Terrell thought that they both just had bad colds, but after a couple of weeks, he developed a severe cough that got "worse and worse," he says. "It progressed to a point that I coughed so deep and so hard that I broke a rib, and it sounded like a large stick breaking. You could hear it all the way across the room."[9] Terrell went to the hospital and was put in the intensive care unit because his difficulty breathing was so serious that he could not even talk. Eventually, he improved and was able to go home, but his disease was not over. He remained exhausted and weak for months. He could not go to work and had no interest in family activities or hobbies. He muses, "I missed out on a lot of good life."[10]

Seven-year-old Daniel also missed out on a lot of life experiences while he struggled with whooping cough. Daniel's mother, Cheri Rae, reports that he coughed so much during the second stage of his illness that she had to sit up with him during the night for weeks. Daniel panicked when the coughing spells left him unable to catch his breath. He vomited at the end of the paroxysms and coughed so deeply that he tore ligaments in his chest. After weeks of coughing and exhaustion, Daniel could not even enjoy his eighth birthday party. He told his mother, "I feel all drummed out. You know how when you play a drum and you use the pom-poms and hit it real hard for a long time until you can't hit it any more, and then you stop? That's all drummed-out. I feel like the drum."[11] After about three months, Daniel entered the convalescent stage of pertussis. His coughing spells occurred morning and evening but not during the day. He had lost 5 pounds (2.2kg), but he could now eat normally again. His chest ligaments healed. Still, whenever the boy heard someone cough, it frightened him. Despite his difficulties, Daniel's case of whooping cough was considered mild by his doctor. Daniel's mother comments wryly that she hates to think of what a *bad* case of whooping cough would be like.

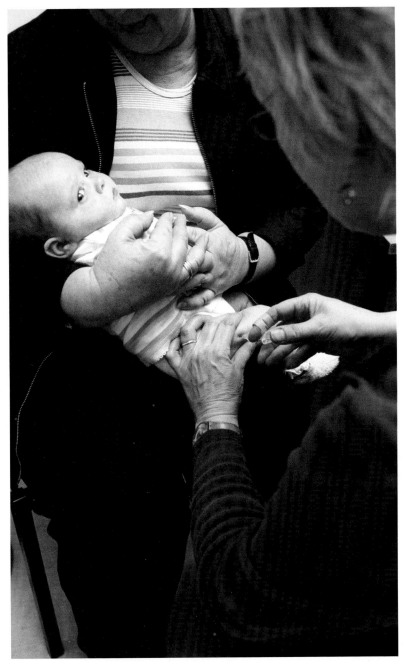

Most people are vaccinated as infants to protect them from catching whooping cough. The protection diminishes over time, however, leading some adults to get a mild case of the disease.

Severe Whooping Cough

Bad cases of whooping cough generally occur in babies and young children and are often life-threatening. Disease expert Dr. Paul Offit explains:

> Children try to rid themselves of the mucus by coughing; but it's so gummy and tenacious that it's impossible to cough up. . . . Coughing isn't the only problem. Some children with whooping cough suffer pneumonia—an infection in the lungs—when pertussis bacteria travel to their lungs, or seizures when their brains don't get enough oxygen, or suffocation when mucus completely blocks their windpipes. Some cough so hard that they break ribs or [for] so long that they become malnourished.[12]

Offit says that young infants are more likely than older infants to die from whooping cough because the young infants have narrower, smaller windpipes that are more readily blocked completely. In developed countries, according to the CDC, more than half of infants under twelve months of age who get whooping cough must be hospitalized. About 1 in 5 of these babies develop

Children with whooping cough sometimes contract pneumonia, a disease of the lungs, when *B. pertussis* bacteria enter the lungs.

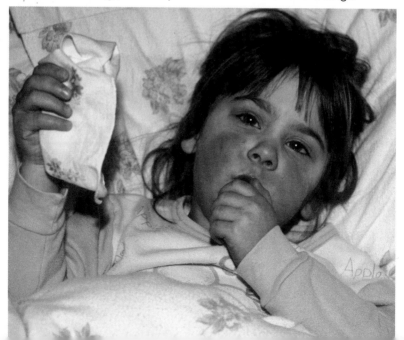

pneumonia; about 1 in a 100 get convulsions or seizures; about 1 in 300 suffer encephalopathy (brain damage) from lack of oxygen, which may be permanent; and about 1 in a 100 die.

Infants can suffer many complications that older children and adults do not because their small, vulnerable bodies cannot handle whooping cough symptoms. Infants do not have the strength to bring up the choking phlegm and to gasp for air successfully. They may cough so much that they are unable to, or just refuse to, nurse. Not eating is dangerous for infants because small, growing bodies cannot tolerate a lack of nutrition as well as larger bodies can. Infants may cough so hard that they bleed behind the eyes or in the brain. They often fail to gasp for air (do not whoop) and simply stop breathing. Even the best medical care may not save their lives.

Dying of Whooping Cough

Brie Romaguera died of whooping cough on March 6, 2003. She was just fifty-two days old. Her parents had taken her to the hospital because she was coughing. While she was being examined, the baby coughed so hard that she turned blue around her lips and passed out. Doctors put Brie in the critical care unit, put her on a ventilator to help her breathe, and gave her antibiotics. Nothing helped, and the oxygen levels in her blood got lower and lower. As Brie got worse, her doctors decided to try putting the baby on a machine called an extracorporeal membrane oxygenation (ECMO) unit. An ECMO unit artificially adds oxygen to the blood of a patient and removes carbon dioxide—a process normally handled by the lungs. Using an ECMO machine allows the heart and lungs to rest and recover. Even this effort, however, could not save Brie. She began leaking fluids into her body tissues and then bleeding into her brain. Finally, the doctors removed the baby from the ECMO unit and allowed her parents to hold and rock her as she passed away.

Landon Carter Dube also died of pertussis in a hospital as doctors fought to save him. He was five weeks old when he fell ill on January 10, 2010. He had trouble breathing, spit up his formula, and coughed. In the hospital, he had so much mucus blocking his airway that the doctors had to suction out his nose and lungs and put him on oxygen. Over the next few days, however, the infant got worse despite every treatment his doctors tried. As a last resort, as was done with Brie, Carter was put on an ECMO machine. His mother recalls:

> I was not prepared for what I saw when I walked back to his room. My sweet baby boy had huge tubes in the sides of his neck while blood pumped in and out of them. The ECMO machine itself required two people to run it at all times. Now Carter had four people in his room at all times, including two full-time nurses and two ECMO technicians. Carter started to swell and wasn't putting out enough urine for the fluid he was taking in. The doctors told us it was related to the stress on his body for being so sick.[13]

The baby's body swelled to twice its normal size. His kidneys shut down completely. Finally, on January 29, the doctors had to tell Carter's parents that there was nothing more they

Doctors use an extracorporeal membrane oxygenation machine (ECMO) on a infant with whooping cough. The ECMO functions temporarily as an artificial heart and lungs, allowing the patient to rest and recover.

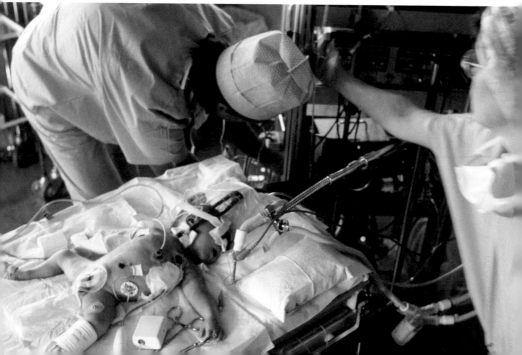

Whooping Cough Spreads

In the Milbrand family of San Diego, California, the spread of pertussis began with the grandmother. She was coughing, but she thought it was irritation from the wildfires and smoke near their home at the time. She did not know that she was a danger to others. When Tara and Grant Milbrand's baby daughter was born, the grandmother's cough spread to the infant when she was just six weeks old. At first, the family thought the baby had a bad cold, but her coughing spells got so bad that she would stop breathing. The infant was hospitalized and diagnosed with whooping cough, but by that time the baby had already passed the disease on to a neighbor's child who had come to visit. This young child coughed so severely that he developed a hernia, which is a rupture in the abdominal wall. Eventually, all three victims recovered from their bouts with whooping cough, but the baby had to spend a month in the hospital, and the older child had to have surgery to repair his hernia that his coughing had caused.

could do. His mother says, "I held his hand, the only thing I could touch that wasn't wired to a machine, and told him that I loved him very much. . . . Carter showed us that he was ready to go to heaven and not hurt anymore."[14] With his parents at his side, Carter died early that evening.

Despite the best available medical care and even when medical experts know what is wrong, infants and young children may be overwhelmed by whooping cough. The danger to the youngest victims is the primary reason that whooping cough is a feared disease today. When small children are infected with whooping cough, modern doctors are sometimes as helpless as doctors of the past, who did not even understand the cause of whooping cough.

CHAPTER TWO

The Cause of Whooping Cough

No one knows how long whooping cough has threatened humankind. In the Western world, physician Guillaume de Baillou provided the earliest clear, scientific description of the disease when he wrote about a 1578 outbreak in Paris, France. He said the disease was popularly named "Quinta" (although he did not know why) and reported that it killed large numbers of infants. In his paper Baillou stated that he had never seen a description of the disease by any other medical writer. One modern-day team of medical disease researchers who have studied the history of whooping cough asks, "Was the disease not known before, or known maybe by other names and in different countries by different names?"[15] The researchers know that a deadly coughing disease was well known in Europe by the eighteenth century and had many names. In Italy it was called "dog's bark"; in Germany it was called "howling of wolves" and "braying of donkeys"; and in English it was named "chincough," which means "howling laughter." Modern medical researchers cannot be sure that all these names refer to whooping cough because until the twentieth century, no one could identify the cause of whooping cough and so could not accurately distinguish it from other diseases.

An early twentieth-century Italian advertisement for cough medicine. There were many names for the coughing sickness, but its causes remained unknown—making it indistinguishable from other respiratory diseases.

The Bacterial Cause

In 1906 two medical researchers at the Pasteur Institute in Brussels, Belgium, were able to determine that whooping cough is caused by a microbe—a microscopic organism. Using a sample of the phlegm of a boy with whooping cough, Jules Bordet and Octave Gengou isolated and grew the bacterium, later named *Bordetella pertussis* (*B. pertussis*), in their laboratory. They proved that infection by this bacterium was the cause of whooping cough by injecting *B. pertussis* into animals and observing the whooping cough symptoms that resulted.

Typical bacteria are living, single-celled organisms surrounded by a protective membrane or protein capsule. Inside the capsule of each bacterium is its genetic material—a single long strand of DNA that codes for how the organism functions and replicates itself. Usually, the size of a bacterium ranges from between one and five micrometers (a micrometer is one-millionth of a meter), and it must be magnified a thousand times under a microscope to be seen. Bacteria can live almost anywhere that they can find food—such as sugars or proteins—and suitable conditions to grow and multiply; they are the most common and numerous organisms on earth. They may live, for example, in soil, on the surface of human skin, on a tabletop, in water, or in the air. Many thousands of kinds of bacteria are known to scientists. Most of them are harmless or even beneficial to people, but some can cause disease when they invade and infect the human body. These are called pathogenic bacteria. Like all bacteria, pathogenic bacteria can multiply extremely quickly under favorable conditions. A bacterium reproduces by fission, or splitting in two; it grows larger, duplicates its DNA, and then divides into two identical organisms. These two bacteria become four, then eight, and so on, until—given enough food and a favorable environment—the single bacterium often has become a colony of millions or billions of bacteria in just a few hours. For pathogenic bacteria such as *B. pertussis* the favorable environment for growth is the moist, warm, food-rich human body.

B. pertussis bacteria are classified by scientists as aerobic coccobacilli. This means that they are a type of short, rod-shaped bacteria that require oxygen to grow and survive. (*Coccus* means

Jules Bordet

Jules Bordet, a physician and immunologist (specialist in the immune system), was born in Belgium in 1870. He became a medical doctor in 1892 and worked at the Pasteur Institute in Paris until he returned to Belgium in 1901 to found a branch of the institute in Brussels. There, he researched infectious diseases and how the immune system works. During his career, he was the first to discover immune system factors in blood, including the existence of specific antibodies to diseases after immunization. With his colleague Octave Gengou he identified a roundish bacterium in the phlegm coughed by a child with whooping cough. (Some historians say that the sample came from his son.) The only way to prove that this bacterium caused pertussis, however, was to isolate and grow it in the laboratory. Figuring out how to isolate the bacterium took six years, but in 1906 the two scientists succeeded in doing so. They injected the bacteria into rabbits and showed that the injections resulted in the disease. The bacterium *Bordetella pertussis* is named in Bordet's honor, and Bordet was awarded the Nobel Prize in Physiology or Medicine in 1919 for his discoveries related to immunity. He died in 1961 at the age of ninety.

In 1906 Jules Bordet, pictured, and Octave Gengou, two medical researchers at the Pasteur Institute, determined that whooping cough was caused by the bacterium *Bordetella pertussis*.

"spherical" and *bacillus* means "rod-shaped.") The bacteria are pathogenic only to humans and cannot live outside a human host. Usually, they invade a host by being breathed into the respiratory tract, after being expelled from another person who has the disease. Once the bacteria are inhaled, they begin to infect the body in stages that generally parallel the stages of disease symptoms that a person experiences.

Toxins Do the Damage

The first stage of infection is called colonization. It occurs before and then during the catarrhal stage of whooping cough. During this stage, the bacteria attach to the cilia, or tiny hair-like structures, of the epithelium, which is the layer of surface cells of the upper respiratory tract. This is their natural environment. In the nose, throat, and trachea, *B. pertussis* clings to the cilia by secreting a sticky chemical.

Some of the chemicals produced by *B. pertussis* are toxic, or poisonous, to human cells. The second stage of infection—

The bacterium *B. pertussis* is seen in an electron micrograph. In the catarrhal stage of pertussis, the bacteria attach to the cilia of the epithelium (the surface cells of the upper respiratory tract).

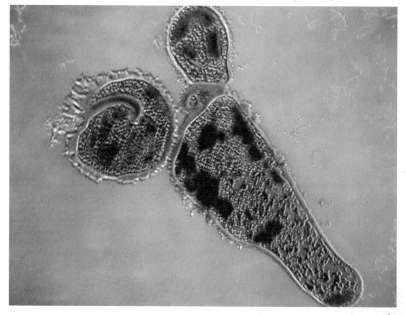

during the whooping, paroxysmal stage of symptoms—is known as the toxemic stage. As the bacteria divide, multiply, and form large colonies, they cling to more and more cilia, damaging the cilia so that they cannot move and clear the airway of the invading bacteria, mucus, and dead cells. During this stage, pertussis toxin is secreted by the bacteria. It not only paralyzes and kills cilia, it also attacks, damages, and kills some of the cells of the human immune system that try to fight off and kill the bacteria. Pertussis toxin seeps into the fluid outside of cells and is carried to other tissues in the respiratory tract, including the lungs. It can even invade the brain via the blood and cause serious damage by inflaming and killing brain cells. In the respiratory system, the toxin causes poisoned, damaged cells to release mucus, and it inflames the airways so that they swell and make breathing difficult. It is not the bacteria themselves but the toxin they produce that causes the dangerous symptoms of whooping cough. Even after the original infecting bacteria have died out from the nose and throat, their toxins that have spread continue to poison and kill cells throughout the respiratory tract.

B. Pertussis and the Immune System

If the symptoms of the toxemic stage do not kill the host, the human immune system eventually is able to clear the bacteria and toxins from the body. The immune system is the body's complex way of protecting itself from infections caused by the invasion of pathogens, or disease-causing agents. It includes specialized white blood cells that detect and destroy foreign invaders. It includes cells that signal the white blood cells called B cells to make antibodies to a specific invader. Antibodies latch onto invaders such as B. pertussis bacteria and signal that they should be destroyed by immune system killer cells. Most invasions by pathogens are stopped by the immune system before any sickness occurs, but sometimes serious infections can overwhelm the immune system because it takes time for the immune system to mount a full defense and battle the pathogen successfully. When B. pertussis first invades the mucous membranes of the upper respiratory tract and begins

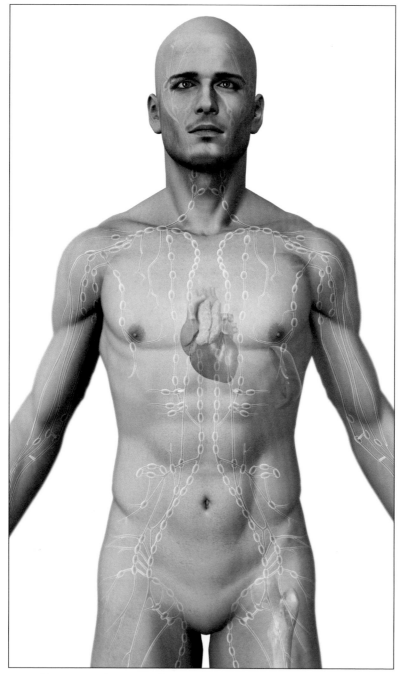

In an illustration depicting the immune system, the heart, the lymphatic system, the spleen, and the humerus bone are visible.

to multiply, the bacteria are immediately recognized as foreign by the immune system. *B. pertussis* is relatively easily killed by immune system fighters, but some immune system cells are attacked by the toxin and killed. This means that the immune system must generate more cells to fight the infection, and that takes time. At the same time, the production of antibodies specific to *B. pertussis* is a process that requires a week or two. That is why a person infected with whooping cough can develop serious symptoms before his or her immune system wins the battle against the invading bacteria, allowing the person to heal. In young infants, this time lag may prove fatal.

Although the immune system can eventually defeat and kill all the bacteria, it cannot change the fact that cilia are already damaged and dead. Therefore, even when the bacteria are gone, the course of whooping cough remains relatively unchanged. The infected person still goes through many weeks of coughing, difficulty breathing, and increased mucus production. The *Gale Encyclopedia of Children's Health* explains: "Symptoms only improve when the old, damaged lining cells of the respiratory tract are replaced over time with new, healthy, cilia-bearing cells."[16] That is why whooping cough symptoms can last up to three or more months. It takes that long for the body to replace all the damaged cilia.

B. Pertussis Continues Its Life Cycle

Not all the *B. pertussis* bacteria that invade a host are necessarily killed by the immune system. Some of the colony of bacteria may continue their life cycle by invading other human hosts. In the early stages of *B. pertussis* infection, when the bacteria are colonizing the upper respiratory tract, some bacteria are released into the air whenever the infected person coughs or sneezes. With every cough, water droplets are released into the air, and *B. pertussis* is in the water droplets. Any person who is close by breathes in the bacteria and is likely to be infected, too. The period during which this transmission from one person to another usually occurs is during the catarrhal stage—the time when the bacteria are multiplying in the nose and throat. People in face-to-face contact with

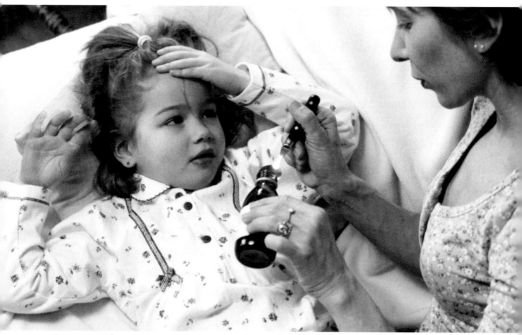

Because whooping cough is contagious, family members of the patient are likely to become infected.

the infected person are those in the most danger of becoming infected themselves. Occasionally, people may also become infected by direct contact with contaminated articles—paper tissues, for example, that have been coughed into and that are wet with water droplets and bacteria. Transmission of whooping cough occurs most frequently among family members because they are the most likely people to come into close contact with each other. In a 2007 study, for example, a scientific team led by Dr. Aaron B. Wendelboe examined how infants are infected with whooping cough. The team reports that "household members were responsible for 76%–83% of transmission of *Bordetella pertussis* to this high-risk group."[17]

Infectious, Communicable, and Contagious

Scientists classify pertussis as a communicable, contagious, disease. It is also an infectious disease because it is caused by a microorganism that has gained access to the body and grown and multiplied; however, not all infectious diseases are communicable. For example, the bacterium that causes tetanus lives in the soil and enters its host directly through a cut or opening in the skin. Once inside its host, the bacterium does not travel to anyone else. It stays inside the body, infecting only its original host. Thus, it is not a communicable disease. A communicable disease is an infectious disease that can be passed, or transmitted, from one infected host directly to another. Colds, influenza, tuberculosis, and HIV/AIDS are examples of communicable diseases. Different communicable diseases may be transmitted from individual to individual through different bodily secretions, such as blood, waste matter, saliva, or—as with pertussis—through respiratory droplets.

The educational organization known as the College of Physicians of Philadelphia notes that there are several factors required for an infectious disease to be communicable. First, there must be a reservoir where the microbe can live and multiply. A reservoir may be the soil, water, animals, or human bodies—anywhere that the infectious microbe can survive. For

The most common means of infecting others with *B. pertussis* is through coughing. The microbes sprayed into the air can then be breathed in by others.

B. pertussis, however, humans are the only reservoir. Only by being transmitted among humans can it survive. *B. pertussis* cannot be passed on to a person from a dog or a cow, for example, and therefore, a human reservoir is a requirement for *B. pertussis*'s communicability.

For *B. pertussis* to be communicable, it also requires a method of transmission, explains the college. The method is the water droplets that are coughed into the air. Then it needs a way to enter the new host, which is the same method by which it left its original host—through the respiratory tract. Finally, the bacterium requires a susceptible host in which to grow and multiply.

Disease Wars

Many scientists say that humans are at war with pathogenic bacteria and that it is a war that humans may never completely win. The medical scientists of the College of Physicians of Philadelphia say that humanity has to be continually on guard against epidemics of infectious diseases because bacteria are "formidable opponents." The college's website explains:

Infectious diseases have been around since the beginning of time, shaping human history and threatening the world's population. In addition to our own immune system that protects us from infection, we have added technology such as vaccines and antibiotic drugs to combat and prevent deadly microbial invasion. While there have been successes, there have also been defeats, creating challenges as scientists continue to understand and control infectious diseases. Despite historical predictions that infectious diseases would wane, new infectious diseases are emerging and old enemies have reappeared and are challenging our defenses. The battle against infectious diseases, once thought to have been won, has only just begun.

College of Physicians of Philadelphia. "Overview: Emerging Infectious Diseases." Health Media Lab, n.d. www.healthmedialab.com/html/infectious/overview.html.

In humans, susceptibility is a lack of immunity or resistance to the infecting microbe. The human immune system is continually and successfully fighting off microorganisms because it is under almost constant attack. Usually, the individual is unaware that an attempted invasion has taken place. The immune system is resistant to the organisms and quickly conquers them; however, humans are, for the most part, highly susceptible to *B. pertussis* bacteria. Whooping cough is considered a contagious disease because it is very easily transmitted from person to person through casual contact. It is one of the most contagious human diseases known to science. (Only the virus that causes measles is more contagious.) As a microorganism, *B. pertussis* is unusual enough and aggressive enough that a full immune system battle is necessary to eliminate it from the body. It takes about two weeks for all required immune system factors to be generated, and during that time, the bacteria can be spread to other people. Therefore, outbreaks and epidemics of whooping cough occur easily. The true cause of whooping cough is not only *B. pertussis* itself but ultimately a susceptible population that provides the bacterium with a continual reservoir in which it can live and spread. Because of this lack of resistance, whooping cough remains a threat to humans throughout the world.

A Reemerging Disease

At one time, whooping cough was a major cause of death in infants. Paul Offit states that "before a vaccine was first used in the United States in the 1940s, about three hundred thousand cases of whooping cough caused seven thousand deaths every year, almost all in young children."[18]

After the first whooping cough vaccine was developed in the 1930s and was in widespread use by the late 1940s, the number of cases of whooping cough in the United States declined dramatically. In 1976 only 1,010 cases occurred in the United States. Since that time, however, the number of cases of whooping cough has steadily increased, and whooping cough is now classified as a reemerging disease. This means that it was once relatively well controlled but is again rapidly increasing in incidence. Diseases may reemerge in a population for several reasons, but most public health and medical experts agree that whooping cough is reemerging because of a decline in the immunity and resistance in the human population, especially in teenagers and adults. Fewer people are vaccinated against whooping cough, and those who were vaccinated in the past may no longer be immune. Immune system memory is lost over time and thus the effects of the vaccine eventually wear off.

What Causes Loss of Immunity to Whooping Cough?

In addition to the decrease in protection from vaccines, fewer people are exposed to whooping cough in modern times, so fewer people have natural immunity to the disease. In 2011 researchers Jennie S. Levine, Aaron A. King, and Ottar N. Bjornstad reported that the reemergence of whooping cough could be caused by the fact that people's immune systems are no longer as frequently reexposed to *B. pertussis* as they have been in the past. The researchers hypothesize that frequent exposure to the bacteria primes the immune system and keeps the cellular memory active. Before a vaccine was available, *B. pertussis* was common in populations, so people were repeatedly exposed to it. This exposure meant that immunity was periodically boosted in people who had been infected in childhood. Today, because most people are vaccinated, the only exposure people have to *B. pertussis* is in the vaccine they were given as young children. These people then go for many years without ever being exposed to the bacteria again. Thus, their immune systems are never again primed, or boosted, and they lose the immune system memory that protected them. This means that should an outbreak of whooping cough occur because of just one infected individual, teens and adults have no immunity and could easily catch and spread the bacteria.

Because of this lowered resistance to *B. pertussis*, adults and teens remain the reservoir for the bacteria and spread the disease to the most vulnerable members of the population—infants and young children. Babies are born with inexperienced immune systems because they have not yet been exposed to many pathogens, and their immune systems have not yet had to recognize and fight off many pathogenic microorganisms. Their immune systems are immature until they are about six months old. The only protections they have against disease are the antibodies passed on to them in the womb from their mothers' immune systems and later from her milk. Infants are also very dependent on the immunity of the larger community into which they are born. They depend on what is called herd immunity to keep them safe.

Herd Immunity

Herd immunity, also known as community immunity, is the protection of a population or community from disease because a high percentage of the population is immune, usually because they have been vaccinated, but it can also result from natural immunity. In this situation, even when some people—such as infants—are not immune, they are protected from the

Symbolized here by a herd of horses, herd immunity—in which a significant proportion of individuals is immune to a disease—is the best protection against whooping cough for infants.

disease because the reservoir—the number of people in whom the bacteria live—is so low that there is little opportunity for the disease to spread. Offit says that herd immunity works the way "a moat safeguards a castle." The moat is the immunity of the community, and the castle is a vulnerable member of the community, perhaps an infant. Offit contines, "The fraction of the population that needs to be vaccinated to provide herd immunity depends on the contagiousness of the infection."[19] Because whooping cough is a highly contagious disease, he says, 95 percent of the population has to be immune for herd immunity to be achieved. Herd immunity is the best protection against whooping cough for infants, but when even 10 percent of the population is not immune, herd immunity is lost. This, Offit and others fear, is what is happening in the United States and in other developed countries around the world. Offit hypothesizes that the increase in cases of whooping cough in the last few decades is caused by a loss of herd immunity, both because some people refuse vaccines for their children and because adults have lost their protection over time. Without herd immunity, he warns, *B. pertussis* can spread without warning among the members of a community, and infants are placed at a higher risk of death from whooping cough.

CHAPTER THREE

Diagnosis and Treatment of Whooping Cough

In 2010 California experienced an outbreak of whooping cough that the state's health officials and the Centers for Disease Control (CDC) declared an epidemic because the number of cases was so much greater than what was normal for a standard year. It was the worst epidemic of pertussis in California since the 1940s. During 2010 the number of people diagnosed with whooping cough reached 9,477, with ten deaths—all infants. By June 2011 there were 1,428 additional confirmed cases. These numbers compared with fewer than 1,000 cases per year in the state during the 1970s, 1980s, 1990s, and most of the 2000s. Most of the infant deaths, says Dr. John Talarico of the California Department of Public Health, were due to the failure of the infants' doctors to make a fast, accurate diagnosis of the disease. He notes that "in several cases . . . the infants were treated only for nasal congestion or mild upper respiratory infection. By the time these infants developed severe respiratory distress, it was usually too late for any intervention to prevent their tragic deaths."[20]

Diagnosis of pertussis can be difficult for modern doctors. As a reemerging disease, it is unfamiliar to many doctors in developed countries. They may never have seen a case of whooping cough and often do not think of the possibility of whooping

In California flyers in several languages urge people to be vaccinated against whooping cough. In 2010 the state's health officials declared a pertussis epidemic.

cough in a sick individual. Intervention, or treatment, can also be a problem because the toxins that *B. pertussis* produces do not respond to antibiotics or other medicines. Yet, early diagnosis and treatment are critical if epidemics of whooping cough are to be prevented and infant lives saved.

The Danger of Late Diagnosis

When six-week-old Tristen Oliver of Merced, California, developed the first symptoms of whooping cough in July 2010, he did not seem very sick. He was coughing, but the cough was not severe, and he did not whoop. His mother took him to the pediatrician, who diagnosed him with an upper respiratory infection. The doctor sent the baby home and told the mother to take the baby to the emergency room if he got worse. He did get worse. He began coughing so hard that he turned red with the effort; he vomited and refused to eat. Tristen's mother took him to the hospital emergency room. She had heard about California's whooping cough epidemic and says, "I told the doctor

I was worried about whooping cough, but the doctor said it wasn't that."[21] The baby still was not whooping, but the doctor gave him antibiotics anyway and sent him home. Still, Tristen did not improve, and two days later, his mother took him to a different hospital. There, she was told Tristen did not have whooping cough and should stop taking the antibiotics. The doctor took an X-ray to be sure the infant did not have pneumonia, said the baby was fine, and sent mother and baby home.

But Tristen's mother knew something was seriously wrong with her baby. Again, after watching the baby cough so severely that he turned blue from lack of oxygen, she returned with him to the first hospital, which now admitted him and then airlifted him to another hospital where he could receive specialized care. There, Tristen was finally tested for and diagnosed with whooping cough. Doctors sedated him, put him on a ventilator to help him breathe, and began the long fight to save his life. Tristen's mother says, "The hospital said he would be there about a month. They said he's pretty bad, but they've seen worse." She now believes that all parents should be aware of whooping cough and fight for an accurate diagnosis. She warns other parents, "Demand a test. Get them on antibiotics. If they are really bad, demand that they be admitted to the hospital. This has been a terrifying experience."[22]

Doctors Need to "Think Pertussis"

An accurate diagnosis of whooping cough, explains pertussis expert and university professor James D. Cherry, can be a problem. He says, "It's a tough diagnosis because the babies, they don't look very sick. They don't have a fever. And they have a runny nose and a little cough."[23] These symptoms are the same as for an upper respiratory infection, such as a cold or other virus. Such infections are common in infants; they are not serious and do not require any special treatment. They are also much more common than whooping cough, so they are the first diagnosis that doctors think of when they see a mildly sick infant. Nonetheless, Cherry and other whooping cough experts warn that in any area where an outbreak occurs, doctors should act rapidly to test for and treat whooping cough, especially in young children.

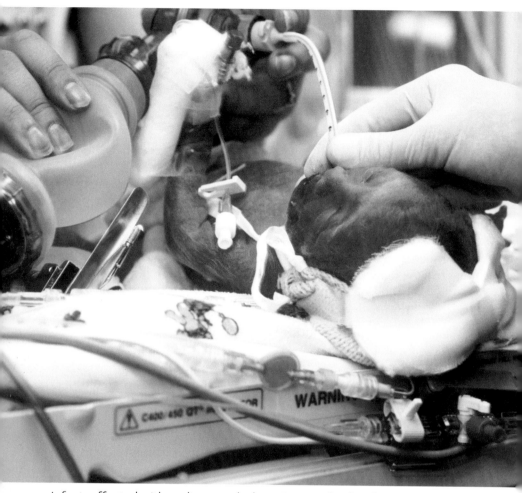

Infants affected with undiagnosed whooping cough often become progressively sicker and may reach such a distress level that they are placed in intensive care to receive help in breathing.

In order to act rapidly, the possibility of whooping cough infection must be in the mind of the doctor who sees a sick patient. Most medical experts agree that diagnosis of any disease is as much an art as it is a science, since so many diseases have similar symptoms. This is especially true for pertussis-infected infants who do not have the distinctive whoop and do not seem seriously ill in the early stages. Because of the California epidemic of 2010, Dr. Jonathan Fielding, the director of public health in Los Angeles County, states, "What we are saying now is that we want those who are seeing these children to think pertussis. We know that early treatment with antibiotics can be life saving."[24] Fielding says that by the time most of the California infants who died were accurately diagnosed, it was too late to save their lives. It is also important to accurately diagnose whooping cough in teens and adults—even when their symptoms are mild—because they are the reservoir from which infants are infected.

Diagnosis of whooping cough sometimes may be made by a doctor simply on the basis of clinical history. This means that the doctor either sees or asks the patient about the specific symptoms of coughing for more than two weeks, whooping, and vomiting after a paroxysm. But a confirmed diagnosis requires identification of the presence of *B. pertussis* bacteria. This can be a problem because, of the two tests currently available, the more accurate test takes a long time whereas the more rapid test is not always accurate.

Pertussis Pete

Although whooping cough has always been considered a childhood disease, doctors have long known that undiagnosed adults (who often have milder symptoms) are a danger to children because they can spread infection. In 1916 a New York doctor reported the case of a man he nicknamed "Pertussis Pete." Pete lived with his sister and her three children. The doctor surmised that Pete caught pertussis from the children. Then he went to visit another sister, and eight days later her children came down with whooping cough. Next, he decided to move in with his brother, and within a week the brother's child got whooping cough. Pete moved again, this time to live with a cousin, and the child in that family got whooping cough. The contagion only stopped because Pete finally enlisted in the military and was shipped overseas.

Diagnosis by Laboratory Culture

The best test for a diagnosis of pertussis, notes the CDC, is a laboratory test called a culture. With this test, the doctor performs a nasopharyngeal (nose-throat) swab. He or she uses a swab on a wire and passes it through a nostril to the back of the throat. It is then twisted and rotated so as to collect material such as bacteria-containing mucus. Cheri Rae, the mother of the earlier mentioned seven-year-old Daniel, calls the swab

A mother cleans her baby's nose with a cotton swab. A similar, but longer and more delicate, flexible swab is used to collect a sample of mucus for laboratory testing for *B. pertussis*.

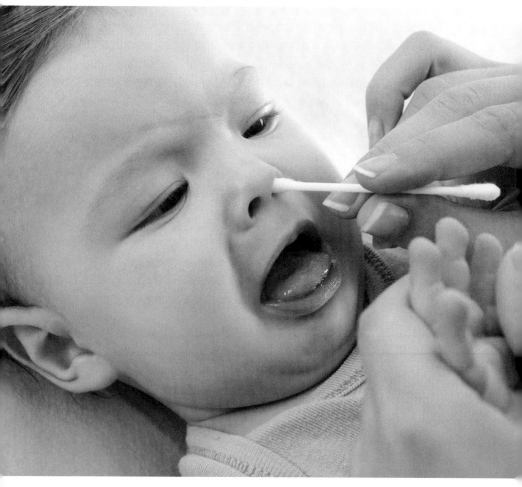

"a nasty little procedure,"[25] but the discomfort lasts only a few seconds. The doctor then sends this sample to a laboratory for testing. In the laboratory, technicians place the swab sample in a dish with selected nutrients and kept at the proper temperature, where any captured bacteria can grow. If a colony of *B. pertussis* grows, the laboratory knows for sure that the diagnosis is whooping cough.

The CDC refers to laboratory culture as the "gold standard" for pertussis diagnosis, but the test has problems. *B. pertussis* is difficult to keep alive and grow in the laboratory because it so specifically prefers the environment of the human respiratory tract. Sometimes, the lab fails to grow the culture successfully. It is also a relatively slow-reproducing bacterium, which means that growing the culture takes a considerable amount of time. The CDC says, "Cultures . . . may take as long as 2 weeks [to grow], so results may be too late for clinical usefulness."[26] Waiting for two weeks to confirm a diagnosis may mean that treatment is not started, and thus the patient gets sicker. In addition, a laboratory culture of *B. pertussis* may not reveal any bacteria if the swab is not taken early in the course of the disease. After a person has been coughing for about two weeks, the body's immune system may already have killed all the bacteria, even though the toxins and paralyzed cilia are still causing symptoms. The bacteria may also be dead if the patient has been taking antibiotics. "Since adolescents and adults have often been coughing for several weeks before they seek medical attention," explains the CDC, "it is often too late for culture to be useful."[27]

PCR Testing for *B. Pertussis*

Because a laboratory culture is so time consuming and may fail to yield results unless the sample is taken early on in the disease progression, many laboratories add another test when trying to confirm a whooping cough diagnosis. It is the polymerase chain reaction (PCR) test for *B. pertussis* bacteria. The PCR is a kind of DNA test. Like the DNA testing that is done to identify particular individuals, DNA testing of bacteria can identify specific kinds of bacteria, as each has its own unique DNA. With PCR testing of the nasopharyngeal swab, laboratory scientists can analyze very tiny samples of DNA by reproducing the DNA and making many copies of the sample. The scientists are then able to distinguish the bacterial DNA from the human DNA and can diagnose whooping cough by identifying the DNA of *B. pertussis*. Unlike with laboratory cultures, the bacteria do not have to be alive for their DNA to be detected.

PCR testing is also quick; the results are available in just a few hours. However, PCR tests may yield false positive or false negative results. A false positive is an indication of disease when it is not present; a false negative is a failure to detect the presence of bacteria when they are actually there. According to the CDC, PCR testing after a person has been coughing for about four weeks can yield a false negative because bacterial DNA may no longer be present in the upper respiratory tract. Taking antibiotics for longer than five days can also cause a false negative. Samples from people who have been exposed to *B. pertussis* but have no symptoms can yield a false positive, as can a recent vaccination. A lack of standardized testing practices can also lead to false results, because different laboratories do PCR testing in different ways that may not always be accurate. PCR testing, however, can be a valuable test for the diagnosis of whooping cough even though it is not absolute. It must be confirmed with a laboratory culture, but PCR is a more sensitive test and may help a doctor to make the decision to begin treatment more quickly.

In trying to identify whooping cough, says Dr. Trish M. Perl of the Johns Hopkins Medical Center, "you don't have a lot of options." Doctors can either choose a test that takes a long time or one that is easy to get wrong. Perl adds, "It's almost like you're trying to pick the least of two evils."[28] Doctors are frustrated by the shortcomings of the diagnostic tests currently available. The CDC says that no single diagnostic test can be counted on to confirm whooping cough in all people. In teens and adults, doctors also often do blood tests to search for the presence of antibodies to *B. pertussis*. In infants, blood tests can identify an elevated white blood cell count that indicates an infection. These tests are like pieces of the diagnostic puzzle

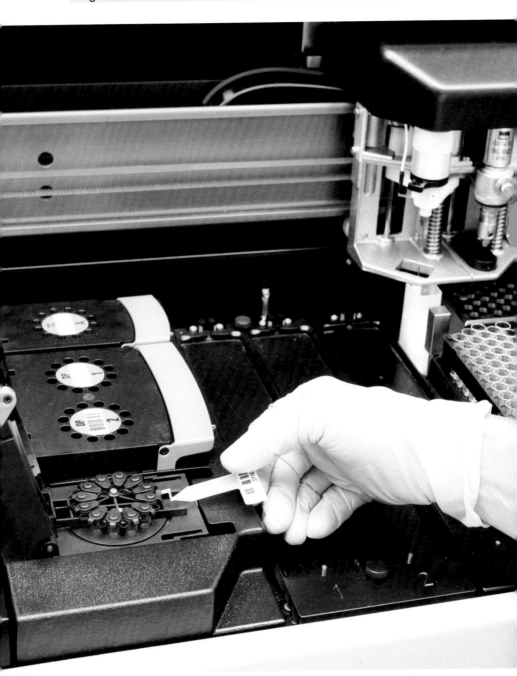

Using a COBAS Amplicor machine, a lab technician runs a polymerase chain reaction (PCR) test. Many laboratories performing PCR tests are successfully diagnosing whooping cough.

that add to the doctor's information. However, not all infants have high white blood cell counts, and the presence of antibodies may simply indicate that the person was vaccinated or had the disease in the past. In the end, a doctor has to make his or her diagnosis based on all available information and the signs and symptoms in an individual patient.

Antibiotic Treatment of Whooping Cough

Even when a diagnosis of whooping cough can be confirmed, medical treatment does not mean a cure. According to the CDC, "The medical management of pertussis cases is primarily supportive."[29] This means that the primary goal is to help the patient survive and be as comfortable as possible while waiting for the disease to run its course. Despite the fact that whooping cough cannot be cured, however, the CDC does recommend treatment with antibiotics for many people with whooping cough, especially if it is diagnosed in the catarrhal stage. During this first stage, *B. pertussis* bacteria are still active and multiplying in the upper respiratory tract. Killing the bacteria at this stage can ameliorate symptoms, meaning that the patient will feel better, have milder symptoms, and recover more quickly. Also, the antibiotic treatment does prevent the patient from transmitting the bacteria to other people. When whooping cough is diagnosed this early, the treatment of choice is the antibiotic erythromycin. This drug is the best antibiotic for killing *B. pertussis*. Other antibiotics, such as penicillin-based medicines, are ineffective against the bacteria. Medical experts are unsure why so many antibiotics have no effect on *B. pertussis*, but they hypothesize that the antibiotics cannot penetrate the mucus lining of the respiratory tract. Erythromycin can and does, and doctors generally prescribe four doses a day for fourteen days.

Once a person is in the second stage of pertussis and suffering paroxysms, erythromycin has no effect on the disease because bacteria are no longer the problem; the pertussis toxins are causing the symptoms, and they are completely unaffected by antibiotic therapy. Nevertheless, most doctors prescribe erythromycin in the second stage in order to protect other people. The antibiotic may not change the course of whooping cough in a particular patient, but it can kill any remaining bacteria and make the person noncontagious within about five days. This treatment is especially important to protect the families of the infected individual—especially any infants in the home. Often, the antibiotic is given to all people in the family who may have been exposed to *B. pertussis*, even when they show no symptoms.

Although there is no cure for whooping cough, the antibiotic erythromycin has been found to be the most effective at killing *B. pertussis* bacteria.

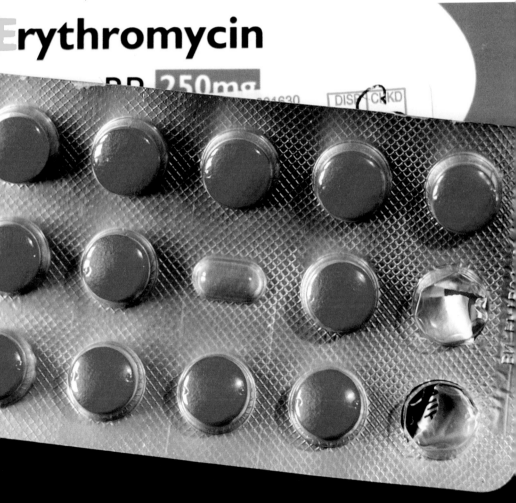

When a treatment is given before it appears to be necessary, it is called a prophylaxis, or preventive treatment. Antibiotics are given as a prophylaxis to control the spread of whooping cough.

Erythromycin, however, cannot be given to infants under about four weeks old. It can cause severe problems in their immature gastrointestinal tracts (the stomach and intestines). The antibiotic can be unpleasant for older children and adults, too. Its side effects include irritation of the gastrointestinal tract, leading to painful cramps, nausea, diarrhea, and vomiting. Many people find themselves unable to take erythromycin for the full fourteen days that are needed. When that is the case, doctors may prescribe one of two other antibiotics that are effective against *B. pertussis*, although not quite as effective as erythromycin. They are called azithromycin and clarithromycin and are used because their associated side effects are milder. These drugs, too, can cause gastrointestinal problems, but the distress is not as likely as with erythromycin. They may also cause headaches and dizziness. In older infants, children, and adults clarithromycin can be substituted for erythromycin. Many people who cannot tolerate erythromycin may be able to take clarithromycin. For infants under the age of four weeks, when an antibiotic is absolutely necessary, only azithromycin is safe enough to try. Even then, these young infants must be carefully monitored for serious gastrointestinal problems for at least a month after treatment is completed.

Supportive Treatments

For children, teens, and adults who have progressed to the second stage of whooping cough, doctors may recommend some supportive treatments to ease their symptoms while they wait to recover. Dr. Tom Clark of the CDC adds:

> Over-the-counter cough medicines are not recommended and don't really help. The prescription medicines that are really effective for cough are pretty strong medicines, so they're generally avoided in young children and probably not effective in pertussis specifically. It's commonly recommended to minimize the things that can trigger the

cough. A humidifier helps. Breathing moist air will help. With younger kids, try to keep them calm and not agitated or running around.[30]

For infants, more aggressive supportive treatment may be necessary. If their whooping cough is severe, these patients may have to be hospitalized, sometimes in intensive care. About 75 percent of babies younger than six months of age have to be hospitalized when diagnosed with whooping cough. Dr. Hazel Guinto-Ocampo explains the goals of the supportive treatment in young children: "The goals of therapy include limiting the number of paroxysms, observing the severity of cough, providing assistance when necessary, and maximizing nutrition, rest, and recovery."[31] The treatment and assistance may include providing oxygen and giving intravenous (IV) fluids when the patient is unable to eat and drink. If the patient is malnourished, nutrition can also be provided through a tube. Infants may need to have the thick mucus suctioned from their airways. Doctors also often prescribe sedatives for babies to be sure that they rest and stay quiet so as to avoid the triggering of paroxysms that could cause suffocation or the breaking of blood vessels and bleeding in the brain. If necessary, treatment may involve a ventilator—inserting a breathing tube down the throat to keep the airways open and help the patient breathe until he or she recovers.

Success Is Not Guaranteed

Treatment must also include avoiding or addressing the complications that can occur with whooping cough. The most common complication of severe whooping cough is secondary pneumonia. This is pneumonia caused by another pathogen that is able to invade because the respiratory system and immune system are so weakened by pertussis. Hospitalization and antibiotic treatment may protect a vulnerable baby from exposure to this secondary invader; however, when the baby is already infected, this microbe must be treated with an appropriate antibiotic. Most of the time in developed countries even young infants successfully recover from whooping cough

Rest and Relaxation for Whooping Cough

The Mayo Clinic provides some recommendations to help people feel better as they recover from pertussis. In addition to getting lots of rest in a cool, quiet room and drinking plenty of fluids, the clinic suggests eating small, frequent meals, as that can reduce the likelihood of vomiting after a coughing spell. Using a vaporizer can soothe irritation in the respiratory tract and help loosen mucus so it can be coughed up. Warm showers and steamy baths may also ease breathing and reduce coughing, because warm, moist air loosens phlegm and opens airways. Since breathing any irritant can trigger paroxysms, the clinic suggests keeping air in the home clean by eliminating such irritants as cigarette smoke or the smoke from fireplaces. Finally, to prevent infecting others, sick people should cover their mouths with tissues when they cough and wash their hands frequently.

Recommendations from the renowned Mayo Clinic for people with pertussis include getting lots of rest, drinking fluids, and using mist vaporizers or steamy baths.

with careful supportive treatment, but medical experts say that the sooner treatment is started, the better. Even with the best care, some infants will die because there is no medicine that can reverse the course of severe whooping cough or prevent deadly complications in all infants. That is why, says Dr. Joseph J. Bocka, "the need for prevention of pertussis through immunization [vaccination] cannot be overemphasized."[32] Prevention, rather than treatment, is the best approach to protecting young children from the dangers of whooping cough.

CHAPTER FOUR

Prevention of Whooping Cough

In 1932 Pearl Kendrick was the chief of the western Michigan branch of the state laboratory of the Michigan Department of Health in Grand Rapids. Working in the laboratory with her was Grace Eldering. Both women were bacteriologists—scientific specialists in the study of bacteria. At that time, their jobs with the Department of Health involved helping cities to establish sanitary practices (such as maintaining clean water and disposing of sewage), providing health education to citizens, testing water and milk supplies for pathogenic bacteria, and screening immigrants to the state for communicable diseases. Kendrick and Eldering wanted to do more, however. They wanted to learn about *B. pertussis* and develop a vaccine to prevent it.

Scientists had already developed vaccines for some diseases, such as smallpox, tetanus, diphtheria, and typhoid fever, but despite the efforts of researchers, no vaccine against whooping cough had ever proved effective. Whooping cough remained a killer. At the time, about six thousand children died of whooping cough in the United States each year. The disease killed more infants than polio, measles, tuberculosis, and all other childhood diseases combined. All that state health departments could do to prevent pertussis outbreaks was to quarantine, or isolate, infected people so that they could not spread the disease to others. Quarantines usually lasted for two weeks. This time span was just an estimate, because no one really knew how long an infected person was contagious. Despite efforts to quarantine patients, epidemics of whooping cough remained almost impossible to curb.

An early whooping cough vaccine. Two scientists, Pearl Kendrick and Grace Eldering, developed the first effective whooping cough vaccine in 1939.

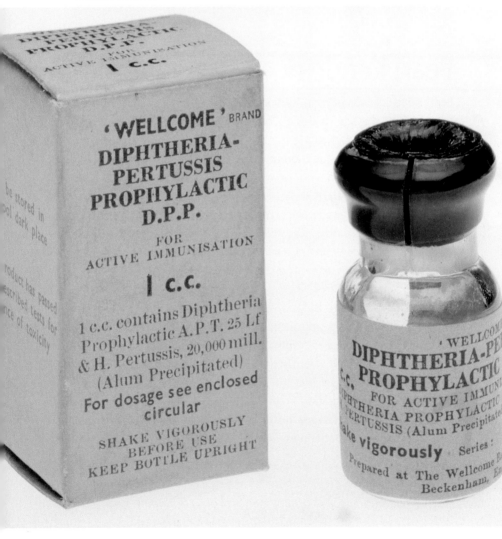

Knowing the Enemy

In 1932 the people of Grand Rapids suffered an outbreak of whooping cough, and Kendrick and Eldering were determined to study it. The Department of Health had no money to support their research, but they were given permission to use the laboratory for their studies once all their regular work was done. The two researchers visited families in which someone had whooping cough and requested samples from infected children by having patients cough on laboratory plates. Nurses and doctors with the Public Health Department collected samples for

Pearl Kendrick

Pearl Kendrick was born in 1890 in Illinois, and she caught whooping cough at the age of three. The little girl survived and grew up to become a teacher in New York. While she was teaching, she continued her own education at Columbia University, majoring in bacteriology. She then went on to get a PhD in bacteriology at the Johns Hopkins University in 1932. After graduation, she accepted a position in Grand Rapids, Michigan, directing the Michigan Health Department's laboratory. She hired bacteriologist Grace Eldering to be her laboratory partner, and the two scientists began their research of *B. pertussis*. After they developed the first effective pertussis vaccine, Kendrick shared her knowledge with scientists around the world and helped the World Health Organization of the United Nations set up vaccination programs in Mexico, Eastern Europe, and Central and South America. Although Kendrick was appreciated by fellow scientists, she never became wealthy or famous for the pertussis vaccine. She refused offers to appear on television and lived quietly in her Michigan home. When Kendrick died in 1980, one colleague noted that "all she did was save hundreds and thousands of lives." And, he added, that fact was her "very best reward."

Quoted in Carolyn G. Shapiro-Shapin. "Pearl Kendrick, Grace Eldering, and the Pertussis Vaccine." *Emerging Infectious Diseases Journal*, August 2010. www.cdc.gov/eid/content/16/8/1273.htm.

them, too. Then, in their laboratory, the scientists experimented with the cough plates to discover the right temperatures, nutrition, and other conditions needed to rapidly grow colonies of the bacteria. Later, recalling that time, Kendrick said, "When the work day was over, we started on the research because it was fun. We'd come home, feed the dogs, get some dinner and get back to what was interesting."[33]

By the end of 1932 they had learned how to diagnose pertussis by growing colonies of bacteria on the cough plates and could use these plates to determine exactly how long a person with pertussis was contagious. They discovered that bacteria were present on the cough plates in enough quantity to infect others even after a child had been sick for three weeks. After four weeks, the majority of the cough plates were clear of *B. pertussis*. After five weeks, 90 percent of the cough plates showed no bacteria. On the basis of this new information about the contagiousness of *B. pertussis*, Michigan began requiring a thirty-five-day quarantine period for those infected, and required that the cough-plate test for *B. pertussis* be negative (or show no bacteria) before a child could return to school.

A Pertussis Vaccine

The next step was to develop a safe and effective vaccine. All vaccines work essentially in the same way. They are preparations of pathogens or parts of pathogens that are made harmless and then introduced to the body and to the immune system. The result is that the immune system is taught to recognize and make antibodies to the pathogen without any danger of the actual disease. The National Institute of Allergy and Infectious Diseases, part of the National Institutes of Health, explains: "Vaccines consist of killed or modified microbes, components of microbes, or microbial DNA that trick the body into thinking an infection has occurred. A vaccinated person's immune system attacks the harmless vaccine and prepares for invasions against the kind of microbe the vaccine contained. In this way, the person becomes immunized against the microbe."[34]

Kendrick and Eldering had learned a great deal about *B. pertussis*, and they believed that they could make a whooping cough vaccine. Kendrick asked her boss for permission to try, and the director of the state laboratories told them, "Go ahead and do all you can with pertussis if it amuses you."[35] Despite his skepticism, the researchers got to work. They made their whooping cough vaccine by killing their *B. pertussis* bacteria with a chemical called thimerosal, which is an antiseptic, a substance that prevents the growth of microbes. Just to be safe they also kept the thimerosal-exposed bacteria in a cold room for a week, because *B. pertussis* depends on temperatures close to human body temperature to survive. They combined the dead bacteria in a fluid, or serum, and then purified it to be certain it was sterile. To test the safety of the vaccine, they injected it into animals and watched for any reactions. Then they injected it into their own arms.

Once sure of the safety of the vaccine, they were ready to test it for efficacy—that is, for whether it produced the desired result and prevented pertussis infection. The researchers recruited volunteers from the families in the Grand Rapids area and injected 712 children with the vaccine. Another 880 children were the control group. These children received no vaccine but were followed in order to determine how many got whooping cough. In 1936 the researchers reported that 45 children in the control group contracted whooping cough, whereas only 4 of the vaccinated children did. No vaccine is 100 percent effective, but this trial suggested an 89 percent protection rate against whooping cough. Kendrick and Eldering now had strong evidence that the vaccine prevented whooping cough in most children. The results were so promising that the federal government granted them funds to do further, larger trials of the new vaccine. By 1939 the researchers had learned that when given in three separate doses, the pertussis vaccine was 90 percent effective in providing immunity from whooping cough and stopped the epidemics that had been so common in the past. By 1940 the vaccine was being recommended nationwide, and by 1948 it was being produced on a large scale by drug companies and was in widespread use. The results were dramatic. In the United States in 1934 the death rate from whooping cough was 5.9 out of every 100,000

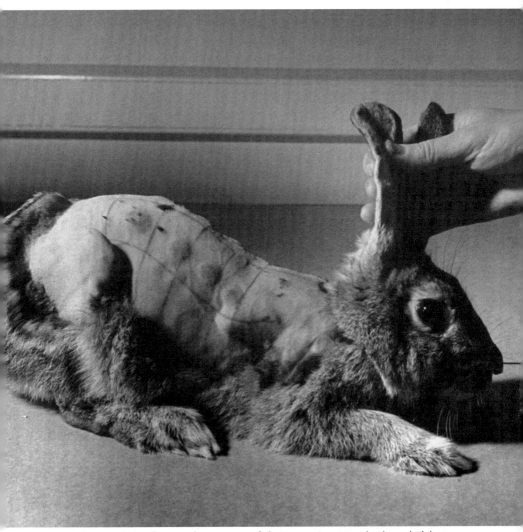

To test the safety and potency of their vaccine, Kendrick and Eldering experimented on rabbits and other animals before injecting themselves with the vaccine.

people. In 1948, this death rate had dropped to less than 1 per 100,000. In 1942 Kendrick and Eldering had combined the vaccine with those for diphtheria and tetanus so that children would have to have fewer shots, and parents flocked to doctors and hospitals to get their children this DTP (also referred to as DPT) vaccine. Pertussis was a dangerous killer no more.

Adverse Events

Despite the success of the pertussis vaccine, it was not without its problems. Because it was made with whole, killed bacteria, the vaccine could cause side effects as the immune system reacted to all the antigens of the bacteria. Antigens are any substances that provoke an immune response and the production of antibodies. Bacteria have hundreds or thousands of these antigens on their surfaces, and *B. pertussis* is known to have more than three thousand antigens on its surface. By the 1970s bad reactions to the pertussis vaccine—known as adverse events—were reported by the Centers for Disease Control (CDC) to be common in young children. Some researchers determined that mild but uncomfortable reactions occurred in as many as 50 percent of vaccinated children. Typically, they included soreness, redness, and swelling at the injection site, fever, drowsiness, fussiness, vomiting, and temporary refusal to eat. Occasionally, however, the side effects could be severe. Children were reported to have convulsions and even suffer brain damage. These serious adverse events seemed to occur in about one in a million cases of vaccination. The CDC was not certain that brain damage could be caused by the pertussis vaccine, but some researchers and parents did worry about the danger.

The Acellular Pertussis Vaccine

Because of these issues with the original vaccine, a research team in Japan under the leadership of Dr. Yuji Sato set out to develop a new, safer pertussis vaccine. In the laboratory, in 1974, they figured out which antigens on the surface of *B. pertussis* were the ones that triggered the antibodies that would protect against infection. They isolated these antigens so that they could be used alone to make a vaccine. The researchers were careful to specifically identify and remove the antigen that causes fever, to diminish the risk of this symptom following vaccination. Then in 1978 they developed a purified vaccine that contained only the important antigens. The vaccine is called an acellular—that is, lacking cells—vaccine because it is not made of the whole, killed bacterium (or cell) but just the bits of the bacterium that trigger an immune response and antibody production. It was tested in thousands of children for safety and efficacy and approved for use by the Japanese government in 1981. In 1984 Sato and his colleagues wrote a paper in the medical journal the *Lancet* that compared the acellular vaccine with the old whole-cell vaccine. They said that "the incidence of fever with [the acellular vaccine] is only 10 percent of that with whole-cell vaccine, and it did not produce febrile fits [fever-caused seizures]. The incidence of local side effects [at the injection site] was also 75–80 percent less than that with whole-cell vaccine."[36] The acellular pertussis vaccine was approved for use in the United States by the Food and Drug Administration (FDA) in 1991. This vaccine is safer than the whole-cell vaccine developed by Kendrick and Eldering and has fewer side effects because it contains between only two and five antigens instead of all three thousand. It is also combined with diphtheria and tetanus vaccines in a vaccine called DTaP, where the small *a* refers to "acellular."

DTaP replaced the old DTP vaccine in the United States in 1996. It is given in four or five doses during early childhood, beginning at the age of two months. Various studies report it to be between 83 and 97 percent effective in preventing whooping cough when all doses are given. DTP is no longer used in the United States, but in many countries it is still used because it is cheaper and easier to manufacture than the acellular vaccine. In many developing countries, where pertussis is a serious threat to infants, the risks of vaccine side effects are much lower than the risks associated with getting whooping cough. Whether with DTaP or DTP, protection against whooping cough is equally strong.

Boosting Immunity

The immunity provided by the DTaP and DTP vaccines is not lifelong, however. Unlike with some other diseases, neither whooping cough infections nor pertussis vaccinations can protect people from ever getting the disease again. In 2005 a research team at the University of North Carolina–Chapel Hill reported that people who have had whooping cough maintain

immunity for about 4 to 20 years. People who have been vaccinated remain immune for only about 4 to 12 years. Scientists
believe that pertussis immunity lessens because the immune
system loses memory over time. This means that outbreaks of
whooping cough cannot be prevented merely by vaccinating
someone in early childhood. Booster shots (so called because
they boost protection) are needed if people are to stay immune
to pertussis.

Mothers in India wait for their children to receive the DTP (diphtheria, tetanus, and pertussis) vaccination. Because the vaccine is good for only four to twelve years, booster shots are needed.

In 2005 the CDC and medical experts recommended a booster vaccine called Tdap for teens and adults; it boosts the immune system's response to *B. pertussis* for about ten years. Tdap protects against the same diseases as DTaP, but in a different formulation for different age groups. Even people who have had whooping cough can be vulnerable to reinfection, so they too need booster shots about every ten years in order to remain immune to the disease. In 2010 the CDC recommended Tdap boosters for older children and seniors (those over the age of sixty-five), as well as for teens and adults. The CDC urges, "Getting vaccinated with Tdap is especially important for families with and caregivers of new infants."[37] Since infants cannot even begin to receive pertussis vaccinations until they are two months old, vaccinating older children, teens, and adults to create herd immunity is the only way to protect them from exposure to pertussis.

Prevention Efforts for Communities

Despite the reemergence of whooping cough, few people in the United States get the Tdap booster vaccination. In one 2008 study, for example, researchers discovered that only about 6 percent of adults had received a booster shot for pertussis. Even among health care providers—who are at great risk of being infected or of infecting their patients—only about 16 percent had received Tdap vaccines. Because of this situation,

The Tdap booster vaccine protects against three potentially deadly bacterial diseases: tetanus, diphtheria, and pertussis. Some experts say the vaccine should be mandatory, to protect the entire population.

some medical experts believe that the way to prevent whooping cough and to protect everyone is to make vaccination not voluntary but mandatory.

Mandatory Tdap vaccinations are already a reality in one state. The Department of Public Health of California and the state legislature have responded to California's 2010 whooping cough epidemic with a new law. Beginning with the September 2011 school year, all students in grades seven through twelve must present proof of Tdap vaccination against pertussis before entering school. The law covers students in both public and private schools and requires that schools exclude any student who does not comply with the law. The California Department of Public Health explains the need for the new requirement this way: "Many schools in California have suffered from outbreaks of whooping cough. Students got very sick and parents missed work and lost wages to care for their sick children. In some cases, schools had to close because there were not enough healthy teachers to keep schools open."[38]

In a few instances, California's lawmakers and public health officials will allow the waiving of the Tdap requirement. For instance, some students may have existing illnesses that make vaccination unsafe. Others may come from families that are strongly opposed to any vaccinations. These students may still be allowed to attend school, but Barbara Woodard-Cox of the Public Health Department says the parents must sign a waiver. She says, "The waiver points out in detail the consequences of the illness and if there's a case in the school, your child may be sent home for three weeks or more because we want to make sure students are safe."[39]

Public-Health Control Strategies

Isolating a student who is unprotected and who may serve as a source of infection is a traditional way to interrupt the spread of whooping cough. In an individual, vaccination is considered the best prevention method, but in a population that does not have herd immunity, a version of quarantine may be the best prevention tool for averting full-blown epidemics when pertussis outbreaks occur. Most state governments and public

Get It for Free

One strategy used by public health officials to prevent whooping cough is to offer free vaccinations to the public. In California, where a whooping cough epidemic is ongoing, county health providers offered free Tdap boosters to older children and teens during 2011. At clinics, shopping malls, churches, and farmers markets, any parents who showed up and asked could get their children vaccinated. State officials hope that these free, convenient booster shots will increase immunization rates and halt the spread of pertussis. In New Zealand the government offers free pertussis vaccines to all health care workers, parents, grandparents, foster parents, and any household members who are in contact with any infant under six months old. The tactics used may be slightly different from those in California, but the reasoning behind the program is the same: Pertussis is increasing among the population and threatening the lives of infants, and free vaccination programs may help prevent the spread of the disease.

Students wait to be vaccinated in California. Because the whooping cough epidemic in California is ongoing, health officials have adopted a "get it for free" strategy in vaccine distribution.

health departments monitor whooping cough cases so as to determine whether isolation regulations or vaccination laws are necessary to protect the community from the dangers of whooping cough. The CDC is responsible for monitoring reports from every state about the incidence of communicable diseases under the National Notifiable Diseases Surveillance System. Pertussis is on the system's list as a notifiable disease. This means that each state and state public health agency reports its cases of disease to the CDC. With this information, the CDC is able to identify outbreaks of pertussis and to evaluate the efforts to intervene and control the spread of the disease.

The state of Iowa, for example, is typical of states around the country. Its laws require all doctors, health care workers, and laboratories to immediately report cases of whooping cough to public health officials. The reports are then turned over to the National Notifiable Surveillance System. Using the information, state officials and the CDC are able to determine when a dangerous outbreak is occurring and to respond without delay. In addition, Iowa requires follow-up of each reported pertussis case. This means that public health officials must visit an individual infected with whooping cough to determine whether he or she is being treated appropriately. The Iowa Department of Public Health usually recommends antibiotic treatment to reduce the chance of contagion. Antibiotics are also prescribed for every person in the family to prevent any possible pertussis infection before it starts.

The Iowa Department of Public Health also recommends isolation techniques for infected individuals. Its manual of procedures states that people with pertussis

> should stay home; this includes exclusion from social settings (e.g., school, child care, work, church, the mall) until they have completed five full days of an appropriate antibiotic. During this time they also should not have visitors. . . . Cases who refuse antibiotics should stay home; this includes exclusion from social settings as above through 21 days after cough onset. During this time they also should not have visitors.[40]

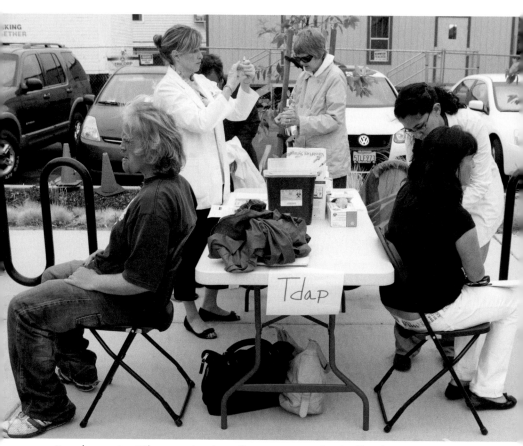

People receive Tdap vaccinations from state medical officials.
Contacts of infected people—who are at risk of infection—are traced
by public health workers, so that they may be vaccinated.

Next, the public health officials investigate the infected person's contacts so they can trace anyone else at risk for infection. The contacts are informed that they have been exposed to pertussis and are urged to get vaccinated, either with DTaP or the booster Tdap. Sometimes, they are urged to begin antibiotic treatment too, especially if they are in close contact with young infants. Finally, public health officials notify all health care providers in the community to be alert to the possibility of pertussis infection in their patients.

Public health prevention techniques cannot eliminate all cases of whooping cough, but the procedures do help to control pertussis outbreaks in a community. Nevertheless, in 2010 Iowa experienced a 229 percent increase in cases of whooping cough compared with the previous three years. According to the medical director of the Department of Public Health, Patricia Quinlisk, 705 cases were reported in Iowa that year. She adds:

> The actual number of cases is probably much higher since most adults with pertussis typically do not seek medical care and therefore are not diagnosed. Most adults haven't had a pertussis vaccination since childhood, so they probably have very little or no immunity left to pertussis. When they get the disease . . . they spread the disease to others without knowing they are spreading whooping cough.[41]

Because so many adults have little immunity to pertussis and because many people are unaware that they have whooping cough when symptoms are mild, the disease can spread in a community despite the best public health efforts. Nevertheless, health officials believe that epidemics would be much more widespread without their public health strategies of containment.

Despite the Best Efforts . . .

In many communities throughout the United States, public health is threatened by increases in whooping cough cases, and public health departments must be continually alert to keep these outbreaks under control. This is true in most of the developed world. In the developing world, pertussis has never been under control, and epidemics are common. Many researchers believe that the only real answer to the dangers of whooping cough lies in worldwide vaccination. That goal has been difficult to achieve, however, both because vaccine delivery is logistically and financially problematic in undeveloped countries and because the value of vaccination is sometimes disputed within the societies of many developed countries.

CHAPTER FIVE

The Future of Whooping Cough

With the introduction of the Tdap vaccine in 2005, many medical experts can see a future without the threat of whooping cough. They believe that widespread childhood vaccinations and regular booster vaccinations could mean the end of whooping cough forever. Pediatrician Cynthia Cristofani of Portland, Oregon, comments, "Whooping cough is a human germ only—no animal reservoir—which means if we can make enough humans immune simultaneously, we could eradicate it from planet earth. Like smallpox, it would be gone, and no one would miss it."[42] The virus that causes smallpox was eliminated from the world in 1980 with an intensive worldwide vaccination program that left the virus with no reservoir. The virus is extinct, and a few other disease pathogens—which also have only humans as a reservoir—may be eradicated from the earth in the future. *B. pertussis* has the potential to be one of those eradicated pathogens. It was almost eliminated in developed countries with the introduction of the first pertussis vaccine. Yet whooping cough is making a comeback, and researchers are no longer sure that they can conquer the disease. This is partly because of the nature of the bacterium and partly because of social issues and concerns that hinder vaccination efforts.

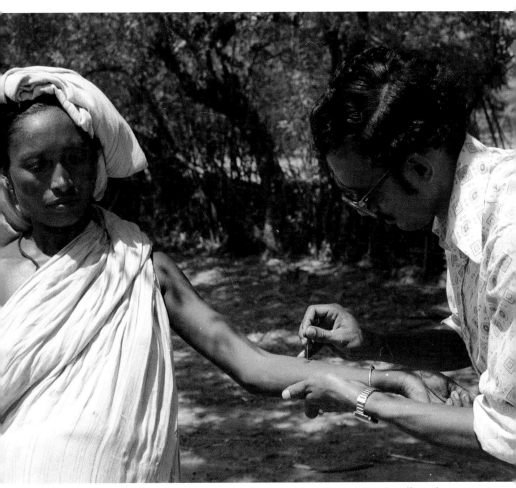

An Indian woman receives a smallpox vaccination in 1974. Smallpox has been eradicated from the natural world through mass immunizations, and experts believe that the same strategy could wipe out whooping cough.

The Anti-Vaccine Movement

Modern researchers want to understand why whooping cough is a reemerging disease and why outbreaks are becoming common in developed countries. Many scientists believe that whooping cough is reemerging because some parents now refuse to get their children vaccinated because they fear that the vaccine will harm or permanently damage their children.

ⓘmmunisation   **NHS**

Going further to protect your child.

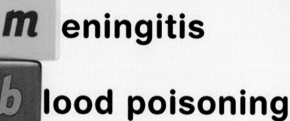

m eningitis

b lood poisoning

p neumonia

e ar infections

Pneumococcal infection can cause the illnesses shown here. Young children are particularly susceptible to it. But up to now, the immunisation programme didn't protect against it. The introduction of pneumococcal vaccine is another example of prevention being better than cure. This vaccine has been used successfully in America for the past five years and some children in the UK have also benefited from it. Meningitis takes a number of forms and they aren't all covered by vaccinations. This additional immunisation will protect against one more sort of meningitis. The vaccine is a single injection and will be given three times: at two months, four months, and thirteen months. And there'll be a catch-up programme for children less than two years old. Meanwhile, you don't need to do anything until you're contacted. Should you have any further questions, ask your local surgery for a leaflet or visit **www.immunisation.nhs.uk**

During Great Britain's 1997 whooping cough epidemic, many parents failed to immunize their children, fearing the side effects. In response, the government launched an immunization drive for pertussis and other childhood diseases, passing out flyers similar to this one.

Fear of the pertussis vaccine began in Great Britain in 1973 when Dr. John Wilson reported that he had identified about 50 children who had developed severe illnesses, such as seizures, blindness, brain damage, mental retardation, paralysis, coma, and death within a week of receiving the DTP (diphtheria, tetanus, and pertussis) vaccine. Wilson argued that these terrible reactions could not be a coincidence and were due to the pertussis vaccine. He said that, in England, about 100 children every year were badly and permanently damaged by the pertussis vaccine. As this report spread to the general public, some doctors and parents in England stopped immunizing children with the DTP vaccine. In 1977, Great Britain was struck by a pertussis epidemic, during which more than a 100,000 children contracted whooping cough. Of those children, 5,000 had to be hospitalized, 200 got severe pneumonia, and 36 died. Many scientists believe that this epidemic was caused by the reduction in vaccination rates, which fell from 79 percent in 1972 to 31 percent by 1977.

Scientists agree that high vaccination rates in a population prevent epidemics, but those in the anti-vaccination movement disagree. The Refusers, for example, are a musical band who are anti-vaccine activists who point out that many people who get pertussis have already been vaccinated. In addition, they say that "Vaccinated individuals can carry the pertussis bacteria and spread it to others. When public health officials blame outbreaks of pertussis on the unvaccinated, they are demonstrating their ignorance about the function of the pertussis vaccine."[43]

In the United States, a television documentary called *Vaccine Roulette* began the anti-vaccine movement in 1982 with reports of damage caused by the pertussis vaccine. The documentary showed several badly damaged children and reported through interviews with their parents that the children had become ill and disabled immediately after receiving the DTP vaccine. The narrator of the documentary, actress Lea Thompson, argued that there were "serious questions" about the safety of the pertussis vaccine and that doctors knew it was dangerous but used it anyway. She added, "The controversy isn't really over the fact that

A Mom Advocates for Protection

Actress Keri Russell has joined the national education campaign known as Silence the Sounds of Pertussis. She is a strong advocate of vaccinations. She tells the following story:

I learned that pertussis, or whooping cough, has been on the rise in recent years, even though it is a vaccine-preventable disease. Following the birth of our son River, I spoke with my pediatrician about what I could do to protect our young child. She recommended my husband and I both get the pertussis booster. My pediatrician explained that parents actually cause more than half the cases in infants, which is why it is so important for adults and adolescents in close contact with infants to be immunized.

I'm partnering with Parents of Kids with Infectious Diseases (PKIDs) to raise awareness about the importance of booster shots for new parents and people who come in close contact with infants. Like any parent, I would do anything to protect my baby, and that is why I followed my pediatrician's recommendation to get the pertussis vaccine myself. I'm very excited to be working with PKIDs to spread the word and help other parents learn how to best protect their babies from this deadly but preventable disease.

Keri Russell. "Protecting Her Newborn from Pertussis." Silence the Sounds of Pertussis, PKIDS Online. www.pkids.org/diseases/pertussis/ silence_the_sounds_of_pertussis/keri_russell .html.

Actress Keri Russell is a strong advocate of vaccination. She has partnered with the organization Parents of Kids with Infectious Diseases to raise awareness of the importance of booster shots in combating whooping cough.

[brain damage] happens, but how often it happens and whether it happens often enough to deem the vaccine more dangerous than the disease itself."[44]

Scientists Respond

It was true that doctors and researchers were aware of the rare dangers of the old DTP vaccine, but almost all agreed that the risks of whooping cough were much worse than the risk of the vaccine. Dr. Edward Mortimer, a vaccine expert at Case Western Reserve University in Cleveland, Ohio, responded that severe side effects, such as fevers that caused seizures, were extremely rare. He argued that "our best estimates are that, of the three and a half million children born annually in the United States, between twenty and thirty-five incur permanent damage as a result of the vaccine. Each of us concerned with vaccine recommendations believes that this is twenty to thirty-five kids too many."[45] Still, Mortimer and other experts believed that many more children would die of whooping cough if there were no vaccine. The American Academy of Pediatrics also rejected the conclusions of *Vaccine Roulette*. It issued a statement that the reporting in the documentary was biased and inaccurate. Nevertheless, fear of the DTP vaccine grew, and it did not disappear when the new acellular pertussis vaccine was introduced.

Between the early 1980s and 2001, many large-scale studies of thousands of children were conducted to look for a possible connection between the pertussis vaccine and brain damage. Each study carefully examined children who had been vaccinated and those who were not and compared the incidence of disability and brain damage. The onset of disability after vaccination seemed to be a coincidence. No connection could be found between permanent brain damage or other disability and vaccination. The children who had been vaccinated and then developed a disability often were found to have genetic diseases that caused seizures, mental retardation, and brain problems. Others had seizure disorders that always begin in the first few months of infancy. Some had caught other diseases. Other studies specifically examined the safety of the aluminum salts added to pertussis vaccines to boost their effectiveness. The National

Network for Immunization Information says that these studies, too, demonstrate no "serious or long-lasting adverse events."[46]

A Future Like the Past?

Despite these scientific studies the anti-vaccine movement, both in Great Britain and in the United States, did not die. The movement and fear of possible vaccine side effects spread to Japan, Australia, and Russia, as well as to most other developed countries, and continues to discourage vaccination of children in the developed world today. Some parents fear that vaccines are unsafe. Others hold religious views against the idea of contaminating the body with vaccines. Still others reject vaccines as unnatural and unnecessary. Some worry that young children get too many vaccines, and some think it is just better to avoid the possibility of problems by rejecting or delaying vaccinations. Many people have not seen the harm that diseases like pertussis can do and believe that pertussis is no longer a danger to their children. Paul Offit reports that as many as 10 percent of U.S. parents now choose to opt out of one or more vaccines for their children. He says that since 1991 the percentage of children remaining unvaccinated has more than doubled; in which case, then, he argues, outbreaks of whooping cough become inevitable, even when most children are vaccinated, because herd immunity has not been achieved.

Dr. Robert Sears worries about the loss of herd immunity, too, but he sympathizes with concerned parents. He comments, "The biggest fear I think every parent has about vaccines is that they don't want their child to be one of those very rare statistics in which their child suffers a very severe vaccine reaction."[47] Sears argues that scientists must do more to gain the trust of society. Without that trust, many health officials fear an uncertain future for the effort to eliminate whooping cough. Cheri Rae is one parent who can understand both fears. When her son Daniel was a victim of whooping cough, Rae learned about the beliefs of anti-vaccination parents. She recalls:

> As one anti-immunization mother explained, "I just don't follow the herd mentality. I just want my children to get

strong and develop their immunities on their own. We don't go to Bangladesh [an epidemic-prone developing country]; we don't have much risk." This approach leaves Rae frustrated and concerned. She says, "As an independent spirit, I'm typically inclined to support alternative lifestyles and philosophies. As a responsible parent, I don't ever want anything bad to happen to my children—or any other children. . . . As a citizen, I am deeply concerned about the impact of health choices made by individuals on the overall health of other individuals and the public at large. Still, the question continues to haunt me: How do we reconcile the issue of maintaining personal beliefs with the devastating reality of communicable diseases?[48]

Despite scientific studies to the contrary, the anti-vaccine movement in the United States and Great Britain has spread to Japan, Australia, Russia, and other developed countries.

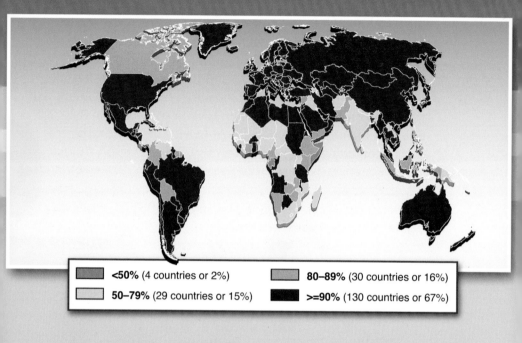

Immunization Coverage with DTP3 Vaccines in Infants, 2010

<50% (4 countries or 2%)   80–89% (30 countries or 16%)

50–79% (29 countries or 15%)   >=90% (130 countries or 67%)

Taken from: WHO/UNICEF coverage estimates 1980–2010 July 2010. 193 WHO Member States. Date of slide: July 26, 2011.

Pertussis Prevention in the Developing World

In developing countries, vaccine fears are not the main problem that makes the future for pertussis prevention uncertain. In many parts of Africa and Asia widespread vaccination efforts have often never been attempted, let alone been successful. Both the cost and the logistics of getting vaccines to undeveloped areas make immunization efforts difficult. The World Health Organization (WHO), the United Nations health agency, reports that 95 percent of the whooping cough cases that occur each year are in developing countries. Since 1974 pertussis vaccination has been part of the WHO's Expanded Program on Immunization (EPI) in developing countries. The goal of this program is to achieve a 90 percent vaccination rate in infants, with a minimum of three vaccine doses in every country in the world. This vaccination rate would protect most infants and young children from severe pertussis infection and greatly reduce the risk of death from pertussis in that age group. Although the goal has not yet been met, WHO researchers and doctors believe it is achievable. The program is aided by pharmaceutical companies, individual donors, private volunteer organizations such as the Red Cross, and foreign aid from developed countries, all cooperating with different governments in developing countries.

The cost of widespread vaccination is one obstacle to whooping cough eradication in developing countries. In sub-Saharan Africa, for example, it costs about fourteen dollars to completely vaccinate a child against six preventable childhood diseases. The DTP vaccine is one of those vaccines, and it is used instead of the DTaP (diphtheria, tetanus, and acellular pertussis) vaccine because it is so much less costly to manufacture. (The other diseases are measles, polio, and tuberculosis.) The immunization cost includes not only the cost of the vaccine itself but also the cost of transportation of the vaccine to remote areas, the refrigeration equipment needed to keep the vaccine viable, and the health providers to give children the recommended doses. Despite the low cost per child, a minimum of $11 billion per year is required to maintain vaccination programs in the poorest countries. In some African countries, for example, it is still difficult and expensive to fly the vaccines to an airport and then transport them to the rural villages where many children live. This effort must be made not just once but year after year if the goal of widespread immunization is to be met. Nevertheless, significant progress has been made. In 2011 the global vaccine coverage for DTP vaccines reached 81 percent, up from 73 percent in 2009. In Malawi, one of the poorest countries in the world, the vaccination rate goal was reached in 1989 and has been maintained every year since. In other countries, however, there is more work to do. The WHO has set the goal of increasing the global vaccination rate so as to reduce deaths from vaccine-preventable diseases by a further two-thirds by 2015.

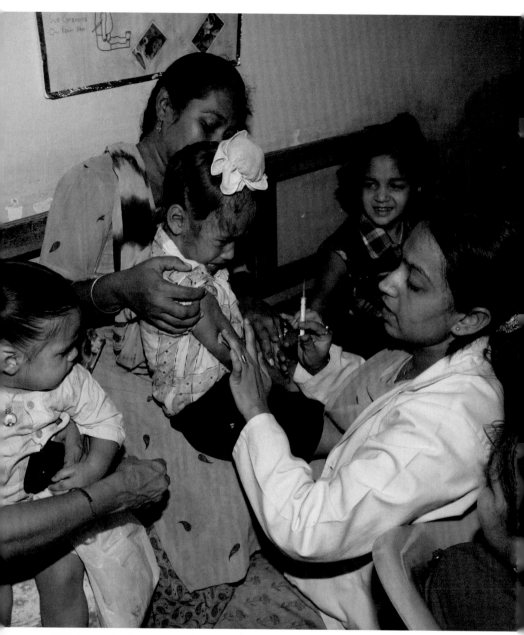

Children in India receive DTP vaccinations. In order for the Expanded Program on Immunization (EPI) to achieve its DTP vaccination goals, the EPI depends on the commitment of developing world governments, backed by the support of the world's wealthiest nations.

Real-World Limitations

Whether the EPI vaccination goals will be successful depends both on the commitment of individual governments in the developing world and the continued support of the world's wealthiest nations. If the 90 percent vaccination rate is ever achieved, whooping cough may become a rare disease in infants and young children; however, *B. pertussis* will not be eradicated. An even higher vaccination rate and continued booster vaccination would be necessary to maintain herd immunity and eventually leave the bacterium with no reservoir. As yet, the WHO does not recommend boosters for older children, teens, and adults in developing countries because of financial considerations. Since immunity wears off as people get older, *B. pertussis* will continue to have a reservoir in populations around the world.

Even if a high vaccination rate is achieved—either in poor countries or wealthy ones—pertussis may not be completely conquerable because vaccines can wear off or may not be completely effective against infection. In developed countries when outbreaks occur, as many as 80 percent of the children who get the disease were fully vaccinated. Although these children get milder cases than unvaccinated children, researchers are still concerned about why these infections happen. No vaccine is 100 percent effective, and occasionally a "vaccine failure" occurs. Dr. Steven F. Hirsch explains: "A vaccine failure occurs when a person who is given a vaccine does not have an appropriate immune response to it, and thus is still unknowingly susceptible to the disease."[49] When herd immunity is achieved (a 95 percent vaccination rate for pertussis), vaccine failures do not matter. A person in whom the vaccine did not work is still protected by the herd. Herd immunity has not yet been achieved in the developed world, however, so vaccine failures may explain why some vaccinated children get whooping cough.

A Better Vaccine Needed?

Of more serious concern for researchers is the possibility that vaccine failure may be caused by a change in the DNA of *B. pertussis*. All bacteria change and adapt to their environments.

Bacteria reproduce and multiply through cell division. During the process of cell division, the DNA is copied so as to produce two identical microbes; however, when DNA is copied, mistakes can be made. These mistakes are called mutations. Some of these mutations are detrimental to the bacterium, some have little effect, and some help the bacterium to survive better. This is how evolution works in all life-forms—organisms with beneficial mutations survive to produce the most offspring and become new kinds of organisms. In bacteria, those of the same species (such as *B. pertussis*) that share these varying mutations are referred to as strains of the bacteria.

Dr. Frits Mooi of the Centre for Infectious Disease Control Netherlands believes that *B. pertussis* has mutated. He has been studying *B. pertussis* in his laboratory for fifteen years and says that he has identified a new strain—called P3—and that it poses a major threat in developed countries. This strain, he says, produces more toxin than regular strains of *B. pertussis*, is more infectious, and is not as vulnerable to the DTaP vaccine. P3, says Mooi, is responsible for vaccine failures because its antigens are different, and those antigens are not included in the DTaP vaccine. Mooi theorizes that the P3 strain surfaced because of widespread vaccination in the developed world. As humanity fought the bacteria with vaccines, the bacteria "fought back" and mutated into a different strain that could resist the vaccine and the immune system's ability to recognize them and make appropriate antibodies against them. That is why, says Mooi, whooping cough has reemerged. Mooi says, "We don't know how effective the current vaccines are against the new strains."[50] Mooi argues that the current DTaP vaccine may need to be replaced with a new acellular vaccine that protects against all *B. pertussis* strains. He wonders if *B. pertussis* will continue to mutate, so that new vaccines will have to be developed regularly in the future. He notes, "The vaccines have less efficacy than many people believe. . . . After all, every year we have a new flu vaccine, so, I think we should have something like that for bacterial vaccines, too."[51]

If Mooi is correct, the future for pertussis prevention seems much less hopeful, but his theories are controversial among scientists. Although researchers recognize that *B. pertussis* has many strains, most are not as certain that the current DTaP vaccine is ineffective against them. Dr. James D. Cherry argues, "There's absolutely no evidence that either of the two vaccines that are most commonly today used in the U.S., that there is increased vaccine failure with either of those vaccines."[52] Cherry, like most pertussis researchers, believes that the disease can be effectively prevented with today's current vaccines, especially if boosters are used to keep most members of a population immune.

A scientist works on developing a vaccine. A serious concern of researchers is the possibility that vaccine failures for whooping cough are caused by changes in the DNA of the *B. pertussis* bacterium.

Cocooning Strategies

No one knows yet whether some strains of whooping cough are more resistant to DTaP than others, but most experts say that today's vaccines are still the best method available to keep people from being vulnerable to pertussis infection. Since infants and young children are most in need of protection, some researchers are concentrating on ways to keep them safe using current vaccines. In 2011 Dr. Gretchen Banks of the Wake Forest School of Medicine reported that hospitals might be able to protect newborn infants from pertussis infection by vaccinating their parents with the Tdap booster as soon as the infant is born. This strategy is called cocooning. It is indirectly protecting infants by vaccinating their contacts. Banks says that up to 35 percent of newborn infants with pertussis caught it from their mothers. About 18 percent got pertussis from their fathers. Banks mathematically analyzed records of infants hospitalized for pertussis over several years. Her results indicated that for every 505 new mothers who are vaccinated, one fewer infant would be hospitalized with pertussis. She says, "Cocooning is a promising strategy to prevent infant pertussis cases. Vaccinating the parents immediately with Tdap post-partum [after giving birth] is an attractive approach."[53] If Banks's recommendations are accepted in the future, many more infants might be protected against whooping cough, even though pertussis remains in the reservoir of the larger community.

Different approaches to cocooning could protect society's most vulnerable members even if *B. pertussis* cannot be eliminated or herd immunity is not achieved. In 2011 the Centers for Disease Control and Prevention (CDC) began recommending that pregnant women receive pertussis vaccine, not to avoid infection but to immunize their unborn children. Some research suggests that mothers can pass on the antibodies their immune systems make in response to vaccination to their fetuses. Researchers are not yet certain that such vaccinations will immunize all fetuses, but studies so far indicate that the infants will be born with protective antibodies. If this is true, infants would be safe from whooping cough until they are old

One Shot for Life

At the Vaccine and Infectious Disease Organization of the University of Saskatchewan in Canada, Dr. Volker Gerdts is testing a new pertussis vaccine. Gerdts wants to develop a vaccine that can be given to newborn infants just once but that will confer lifelong immunity against whooping cough. The vaccine he and his team are developing is made of live, but much weakened, bacteria that can trigger antibody production but are too helpless to cause disease. It is a nasal spray instead of an injection, so it can be applied to the mucous membranes of the respiratory tract where *B. pertussis* invades. Gerdts's team also has added chemicals called adjuvants to the vaccine serum to boost an infant's immature immune system response. The new pertussis vaccine is not ready for people yet. Gerdts and his team are still testing it on animals to be sure it is safe and effective. If all goes well, however, they hope to begin their first human tests of the single-dose vaccine by 2016.

enough to be vaccinated themselves. The CDC also recommends that all health care providers (such as doctors and nurses) receive the Tdap vaccine every ten years to avoid the risk of infecting their younger patients.

The Future Remains Unknown

Since prevention of a disease is always better than trying to treat it, the most important goals for pertussis today are better control of outbreaks and the reduction of the risk of infection in infants. In 1975 Pearl Kendrick asked, "Can whooping cough be eradicated?"[54] What looked so possible then seems less likely now. Although scientists and medical researchers believe the potential for eradication still exists, the future for this highly contagious disease remains unclear.

Notes

Introduction: The Hundred-Day Cough

1. Margaret Morris. "Whooping It Up—Whooping Cough in Chapel Hill." Chapel Hill Children's Clinic: Perils of Parenting, n.d. www.chapelhillchildrensclinic.com/perils-whoopingcough.html.
2. Shot By Shot.org. "Samantha's Story." Pertussis: Story Gallery, n.d. http://shotbyshot.org/pertussis/samanthas-story/.

Chapter One: What Is Whooping Cough?

3. HeyJude74. "I Have Whooping Cough/Pertussis." "I Have Whooping Cough" Experience Project, March 5, 2009. www.experienceproject.com/stories/Have-Whooping-Cough/475977.
4. HeyJude74. "I Have Whooping Cough/Pertussis."
5. Quoted in "What Is Pertussis?" (video). SoundsofPertussis.org. www.soundsofpertussis.org/#/whatispertussis.
6. Centers for Disease Control and Prevention. "Clinicians, Pertussis (Whooping Cough): Clinical Features," August 26, 2010. www.cdc.gov/pertussis/clinical/features.html.
7. Mayo Clinic Staff. "Symptoms: Whooping Cough," December 22, 2009. www.mayoclinic.com/health/whooping-cough/DS00445/DSECTION=symptoms.
8. Quoted in Charlotte Dovey. "Return of the Killer Cough." *Daily Mail* (London), April 17, 2007. www.dailymail.co.uk/health/article-395128/Return-killer-cough.html.
9. Terrell. "Real Stories: Terrell" (video). HelpPreventWhoopingCough.com. GlaxoSmithKline. www.helppreventwhoopingcough.com/real-stories.html.
10. Terrell. "Real Stories: Terrell."
11. Quoted in Cheri Rae. "Hundred-Day Hack: Whooping Cough Takes Hold in Santa Barbara." Parents PACK, The Children's Hospital of Philadelphia, August 2005. Reprinted

from *Santa Barbara Independent*. "Sharing Personal Stories: Whooping Cough." www.chop.edu/service/parents-possessing-accessing-communicating-knowledge-about-vaccines/sharing-personal-stories/whooping-cough.html.

12. Paul A. Offit. *Deadly Choices: How the Anti-Vaccine Movement Threatens Us All*. New York: Basic Books, 2011, p. xiii.

13. Victims of Vaccine-Preventable Disease. "In the Words of Landon Carter Dube's Mother." VaccinateYourBaby.org/ Every Child by Two (ECBT), 2010. www.vaccinateyourbaby .org/why/victims-landon-carter-dube.cfm.

14. Victims of Vaccine-Preventable Disease. "In the Words of Landon Carter Dube's Mother."

Chapter Two: The Cause of Whooping Cough

15. Florens G.A. Versteegh, Joop F.P. Schellekens, André Fleer, and John J. Roord. "Pertussis: A Concise Historical Review Including Diagnosis, Incidence, Clinical Manifestations and the Role of Treatment and Vaccination in Management." *Reviews in Medical Microbiology*, vol. 16, no. 3, 2005, p. 79. www.sepeap.org/archivos/pdf/9902.pdf.

16. Rosalyn Carson-DeWitt, Tish Davidson, and Paul Checchia. "Whooping Cough." In *The Gale Encyclopedia of Children's Health: Infancy Through Adolescence*. Ed. Jacqueline L. Longe. 2nd ed. Vol. 4. Detroit: Gale Cengage, 2011, p. 2,339.

17. Aaron M. Wendelboe et al. "Transmission of *Bordetella Pertussis* to Young Infants." *Pediatric Infectious Disease Journal*, April 2007, p. 293. www.adacelvaccine.com/pdf/ Wendelboe.pdf.

18. Offit. *Deadly Choices*, p. xii.

19. Offit. *Deadly Choices*, p. xvii.

Chapter Three: Diagnosis and Treatment of Whooping Cough

20. Quoted in Rong-Gong Lin II. "Diagnoses Lagged in Baby Deaths." *Los Angeles Times*, September 7, 2010. http://articles .latimes.com/2010/sep/07/local/la-me-whooping-cough-201 00907.

21. Quoted in Carol Reiter. "Elusive Diagnosis: Infant with Whooping Cough Fighting for His Life." *Merced (CA) Sun-Star*, July 24, 2010. www.mercedsunstar.com/2010/07/24/1505770/elusive-diagnosis-infant-with.html.

22. Quoted in Carol Reiter. "Elusive Diagnosis."

23. Quoted in Lin II, "Diagnoses Lagged in Baby Deaths."

24. Quoted in John Hartung. "Diagnosis Slow in 8 CA Whooping Cough Deaths." KABC-TV Los Angeles, September 7, 2010. http://abclocal.go.com/kabc/story?section=news/health&id=7655148.

25. Rae. "Hundred-Day Hack."

26. W. Atkinson, S. Wolfe, and J. Hamborsky, eds. *Epidemiology and Prevention of Vaccine-Preventable Diseases*. 12th ed. Washington, DC: Public Health Foundation, 2011, p. 217. www.cdc.gov/vaccines/pubs/pinkbook/downloads/pert.pdf.

27. Atkinson, Wolfe, and Hamborsky. *Epidemiology and Prevention of Vaccine-Preventable Diseases*, p. 217.

28. Quoted in Gina Kolata. "Faith in Quick Test Leads to Epidemic That Wasn't." *New York Times*, January 22, 2007. http://query.nytimes.com/gst/fullpage.html?res=9501E7DB1F30F931A15752C0A9619C8B63&pagewanted=all.

29. Atkinson, Wolfe, and Hamborsky, eds. *Epidemiology and Prevention of Vaccine-Preventable Diseases*, p. 218.

30. Quoted in Stephanie Watson. "Whooping Cough: What You Need to Know: An Interview with CDC Infectious Disease Expert Tom Clark." *Children's Health*, WebMD Feature, July 19, 2010, p. 2. http://children.webmd.com/features/whooping-cough-what-you-need-to-know.

31. Hazel Guinto-Ocampo. "Pediatric Pertussis Treatment & Management: Medical Care." Medscape Reference, updated May 26, 2011. http://emedicine.medscape.com/article/967268-treatment.

32. Joseph J. Bocka, "Pertussis in Emergency Medicine: Medication." Medscape Reference, updated May 26, 2009. http://emedicine.medscape.com/article/803186-medication#showall.

Chapter Four: Prevention of Whooping Cough

33. Quoted in Carolyn G. Shapiro-Shapin. "'A Whole Community Working Together': Pearl Kendrick, Grace Eldering,

and the Grand Rapids Pertussis Trials, 1932–1939." *Michigan Historical Review*, Spring 2007, p.2. http://findarticles .com/p/articles/mi_7021/is_1_33/ai_n28475194/?tag=mantle_skin;content.

34. National Institute of Allergy and Infectious Diseases. "Understanding the Immune System: How It Works." U.S. Department of Health and Human Services, NIH Publication No. 07-5423, September 2007, pp. 27–28.

35. Quoted in Carolyn G. Shapiro-Shapin. "Pearl Kendrick, Grace Eldering, and the Pertussis Vaccine." *Emerging Infectious Diseases Journal*, August 2010. www.cdc.gov/eid/ content/16/8/1273.htm.

36. Quoted in Harris Livermore Coulter and Barbara Loe Fisher. *A Shot in the Dark*. New York: Avery, 1991, p. 208.

37. Centers for Disease Control and Prevention. "Pertussis (Whooping Cough): Prevention," January 20, 2011. www.cdc .gov/pertussis/about/prevention.html.

38. California Department of Public Health. "Shots for School: FAQs for Parents." March 25, 2011. http://shotsforschool .org/parents_faq.html#requirements-and-documentation-4.

39. Quoted in Susan Abram. "Whooping Cough 'Epidemic' Spurs Drive for Inoculations." *Los Angeles Daily News*, June 19, 2011. www.dailynews.com/news/ci_18312387.

40. Iowa Department of Public Health. "Pertussis Chapter." In *IDPH EPI Manual*, June 2010. www.idph.state.ia.us/idph_ universalhelp/main.aspx?system=IdphEpiManual&context=Pertussis_chapter.

41. Quoted in Robert Herriman. "Iowa Report: Big Increases in Mumps, Pertussis." Outbreak News, July 12, 2010. http:// outbreaknews.com/2011/07/12/iowa-report-big-increases-mumps-pertussis/.

Chapter Five: The Future of Whooping Cough

42. Cynthia Cristofani, "Interview." Edited transcript. *Frontline*. PBS, April 1, 2010. www.pbs.org/wgbh/pages/frontline/ vaccines/interviews/cristofani.html.

43. The Refusers. "Pertussis Vaccine Failure and the Failure of

Pseudo-Scientific Vaccination Policy." Newsroom, The Refusers, September 20, 2011. http://therefusers.com/refusers-newsroom/pertussis-vaccine-failure-and-the-failure-of-pseudo-scientific-vaccination-policy/.

44. Quoted in Offit. *Deadly Choices*, p. 3.

45. Quoted in Offit. *Deadly Choices*, p. 11.

46. National Network for Immunization Information. "Aluminum Adjuvants in Vaccines." Immunization Issues, November 7, 2008. www.immunizationinfo.org/issues/vaccine-components/aluminum-adjuvants-vaccines.

47. Quoted in *Frontline*. "Interview: Robert W. Sears, MD." The Vaccine War, PBS, April 27, 2010. www.pbs.org/wgbh/pages/frontline/vaccines/interviews/sears.html.

48. Rae. "Hundred-Day Hack."

49. Steven F. Hirsch. "Protecting the 'Herd': Why Vaccinations Still Matter." Washington Parent.com, August 2007. www.washingtonparent.com/articles/0708/immunize.html.

50. Quoted in Joanne Faryon. "Investigating an Epidemic." KPBS San Diego, December 13, 2010. www.kpbs.org/news/2010/dec/13/investigating-epidemic/.

51. Quoted in Joanne Faryon and Kevin Crowe. "Immunized People Getting Whooping Cough, Experts Spar Over New Strain." KPBS San Diego, December 14, 2010. www.kpbs.org/news/2010/dec/14/immunized-people-getting-whooping-cough-experts-sp/.

52. Joanne Faryon. "When Immunity Fails: The Whooping Cough Epidemic." Interview, KPBS San Diego, December 16, 2010. www.kpbs.org/videos/2010/dec/16/4972/.

53. Quoted in *Infectious Disease News*. "Vaccinating Parents with Tdap May Lower Rate of Infant Pertussis Hospitalizations," June 1, 2011. www.infectiousdiseasenews.com/article.aspx?id=84811.

54. Quoted in John B. Robbins. "Pertussis in Adults: Introduction." *Clinical Infectious Diseases*. Supplement 2, June 1999, p. S91. http://cid.oxfordjournals.org/content/28/Supplement_2/S91.full.pdf.

Glossary

acellular: Not containing cells.

antibiotic: A medicine that inhibits the growth of or kills bacteria.

antibody: A protein generated by immune system B cells that identifies and binds to a specific antigen to signal that it should be destroyed by other immune system cells.

antigen: Any foreign substance that triggers an immune system response and the production of antibodies.

apnea: From the Greek for "no breath," a condition when someone stops breathing for seconds at a time.

cilia: Tiny hair-like structures on the surface cells of the respiratory tract that beat in a rhythmic motion in order to remove mucus and debris and keep the airway clear.

cocooning: The vaccination strategy of immunizing family members and close contacts of a newborn infant, who is thus enveloped in a cocoon of protection from pertussis infection.

contagious: Capable of being easily transmitted from one individual to another.

DNA: Deoxyribonucleic acid. The chemical molecule that carries the genetic information of a cell and provides the coding instructions for an organism's structure and functions.

DTaP: Diphtheria, tetanus, and acellular pertussis vaccine.

DTP: Diphtheria, tetanus, and pertussis vaccine.

epidemic: A widespread occurrence of an infectious disease in a particular community or population over a given period of time.

epithelium: The protective top layer of cells lining certain tissues of the body.

herd immunity: The protection of a whole community from an infectious disease because enough individuals are immune that the infection of one individual cannot spread to others or cause an epidemic.

immune system: The complex system of the body that defends against foreign substances, infections, and disease.

infectious disease: A disease caused by a microbe that can be transmitted from one host to another.

microbe: A microscopic living organism, such as a bacterium or virus.

mucous membrane: The thin tissue that lines the surfaces of body passages, such as the respiratory tract, and secretes slippery mucus.

mutation: A permanent change in the DNA of an organism that can be passed on to, or inherited by, subsequent generations.

nasopharyngeal: Having to do with the nose and throat.

paroxysm: A sudden fit or attack of disease symptoms that nearly overwhelms the victim.

pathogen: A disease-causing organism.

pathogenic: Disease-causing.

prophylaxis: A treatment that is meant to be preventive, not curative.

quarantine: A period of time during which a person exposed to or infected with a contagious disease is isolated and kept apart from other people so as to prevent the spread of disease.

reemerging disease: Any infectious disease that had declined or been brought under control in a population and is now increasing or resurging in that population.

reservoir: For pathogens, the place in which they can survive. The reservoir may be people, animals, soil, or water—anywhere that the pathogen naturally lives and multiplies.

respiratory tract: The passages through which air enters and leaves the body, including the nose, pharynx, trachea, bronchial tubes, and lungs.

Tdap: Tetanus, diphtheria, and acellular pertussis booster vaccine.

toxin: Any of the poisonous substances produced by some infecting microorganisms.

vaccine: A preparation of killed or weakened pathogenic microorganisms or their parts or DNA that stimulates the immune system to generate antibodies without causing the disease.

Organizations to Contact

Centers for Disease Control and Prevention (CDC)
1600 Clifton Rd.
Atlanta, GA 30333
Phone: (800) 232-4636
Website: www.cdc.gov

The CDC provides extensive information about pertussis for the general public, young people, and health professionals. Additionally, it offers the latest vaccine information and current immunization recommendations.

National Foundation for Infectious Diseases (NFID)
4733 Bethesda Ave., Ste. 750
Bethesda, MD 20814
Phone: (301) 656-0003
Website: www.nfid.org

NFID is a nonprofit organization dedicated to educating the public and health care professionals about the cause, treatment, and prevention of infectious disease.

National Network for Immunization Information (NNii)
301 University Blvd.
Galveston, TX 77555-0350
Phone: (409) 772-0199
Website: www.immunizationinfo.org

The NNii is an affiliation of several medical and health care organizations dedicated to providing scientifically accurate information and education about immunizations.

National Vaccine Information Center
407 Church St., Ste. H, Vienna, VA 22180
Phone: (703) 938-0342

E-mail: contactNVIC@gmail.com
Website: www.nvic.org

NVIC is a nonprofit, consumer-led organization dedicated to ensuring the safety of vaccines and the rights of all people to informed consent about immunizations. The organization says that it is neither for nor against vaccination but does work to prevent vaccine injuries through public education and to monitor vaccine research and legislation.

World Health Organization (WHO)
Avenue Appia 20
1211 Geneva 27
Switzerland
Phone: + 41 22 791 21 11
Website: www.who.int/en

The WHO provides up-to-date information about many infectious diseases, including pertussis, and offers regular reports on its surveillance, global vaccination efforts, assessments of interventions by country, and any outbreaks occurring throughout the world.

For More Information

Books

Toney Allman. *Vaccine Research*. Inside Science series. San Diego: ReferencePoint, 2011. This book explores what vaccines are, how different kinds of vaccines are developed for different pathogens, and how vaccines are researched, tested, and approved for use.

Patrick G. Guilfoile. *Whooping Cough*. Deadly Diseases and Epidemics series. New York: Chelsea House, 2010. The author explores the history of whooping cough, as well as the biology, the toxins, and the treatment and prevention of this reemerging disease.

Noel Merino, ed. *Should Vaccinations Be Mandatory?* At Issue series. Detroit: Greenhaven, 2010. Different authors argue the pros and cons of mandatory vaccinations for school attendance from varying viewpoints, whether the issue is safety, personal freedom, religious rights, or social responsibility.

Noel Marino, ed. *Vaccines*. Introducing Issues with Opposing Viewpoints series. Detroit: Greenhaven, 2011. In a series of articles and essays, this book explores the arguments for and against vaccine safety, effectiveness, and usefulness.

Joseph Panno. *Immune System: Nature's Way of Fighting Diseases*. New Biology series. New York: Facts On File, 2012. This book explores the fascinating, complex functions of the immune system and how it protects the body against foreign invasion.

Websites

5Min Life Videopedia (www.5min.com/Video/The-Difference-Between-Child-and-Adult-Whooping-Cough-326711283). "The Difference Between Child and Adult Whooping Cough." Doctors discuss and play the sounds of a severe whoop in a child and an adult in this short video.

Help Prevent Whooping Cough (www.helppreventwhoop
ingcough.com/index.html). The pharmaceutical company
GlaxoSmithKline funds this site where visitors can find an
interactive map documenting whooping cough cases by
state, watch whooping cough stories from real patients, and
take a quiz on the facts about whooping cough.

NHS Choices (www.nhs.uk/Planners/vaccinations/Pages/science
vaccinations.aspx). "Vaccinations." This site from the United
Kingdom's National Health Service presents two animations
that explain herd immunity and the value of widespread immunization programs for preventing and eventually eliminating disease.

The Sounds of Coughing: An Auditory Guide (http://children
.webmd.com/pertussis-whooping-cough-10/coughing-sounds).
"Pertussis and Whooping Cough? Not on Mom's Watch." At
this site from WebMD, visitors can listen to and compare the
sound of the whoop of pertussis with other kinds of coughs.

Sounds of Pertussis (www.soundsofpertussis.com/#/home
page). Introduced by National Association for Stock Car
Auto Racing (NASCAR) champion Jeff Gordon, the short
videos on this website urge the need for pertussis vaccination to protect young children.

Virtual Museum of Bacteria (www.bacteriamuseum.org). At
this site, visitors can learn about pathogenic bacteria, read
about how the immune system fights bacterial invaders, find
specific information about *Bordetella pertussis*, and see
photos of the bacteria under the microscope.

Index

Picture Credits

About the Author

Toney Allman holds a bachelor of science degree from Ohio State University and a master of arts degree from the University of Hawaii. She currently lives in Virginia and has written more than thirty nonfiction books for students on a variety of medical and scientific topics.